SCIENCE, TECHNOLOGY, AND SOCIETY

THE UNIVERSITY AND MILITARY RESEARCH

Moral Politics at M.I.T.

THE UNIVERSITY AND MILITARY RESEARCH

Moral Politics at M.I.T.

DOROTHY NELKIN

Cornell University Press

ITHACA AND LONDON

355.07
N41 u

First published 1972 by Cornell University Press.
Published in the United Kingdom by
Cornell University Press Ltd.,
2-4 Brook Street, London W1Y 1AA.

International Standard Book Number 0-8014-0711-7
Library of Congress Catalog Card Number 74-38285

PRINTED IN THE UNITED STATES OF AMERICA
BY VAIL-BALLOU PRESS, INC.

*Librarians: Library of Congress cataloging information
appears on the last page of the book.*

To Mark

Acknowledgments

Most of the reports, position papers, and correspondence that document this study are unpublished and were available only through the cooperation of participants in the controversy at M.I.T. during 1969–1970. Those interviewed included L. E. Beckley, Philip Bowditch, Charles Stark Draper, Albert G. Hill, Jonathan Kabat, Elliot Lieb, Charles L. Miller, Philip Myers, Joseph O'Connor, Joel Orlen, Peter Ortoleva, Ira Rubenzahl, Jack Ruina, Vigdor Teplitz, and Walter Wrigley. Others preferred to remain unnamed. The documents they provided and their patient cooperation during interviews are warmly appreciated. In addition, the editors of *Thursday* and *The Tech* are acknowledged for giving access to back issues of their newspapers.

Detailed criticism of an early draft of the manuscript was provided by Harvey Brooks, Noam Chomsky, Franklin A. Long, Paul S. Hohenberg, Mark S. Nelkin, Jack Ruina, Martin Sherwin, Constantine Simonides, and Eugene Skolnikoff. Their criticism, much of it philosophical as well as substantive, was invaluable in checking accuracy, in maintaining balance, and in providing additional information and new perspectives on the events and issues in the case. I also wish to thank Sharon Bryan,

Marilyn Howell, and Maryann Rygiel for their editorial work and for their assistance in preparing the manuscript for publication.

I am indebted to the National Science Foundation for support in the research and writing of this study.

DOROTHY NELKIN

Ithaca, New York

Contents

Tables

Introduction

Universities today are grappling with unresolved issues. These issues are their life blood: . . . students' discontent with the current educational process; the relation of the university to society; the consequences of scientific and technological progress. . . . Particularly, for a great institute of technology, we have the hard question of how our capabilities relate to the defense of the nation. We struggle these days with that issue in its most emotional form, at a time when this country is fighting a war in which few of our students and faculty believe.[1]

On May 20, 1970, Howard W. Johnson, president of the Massachusetts Institute of Technology, announced to his faculty that the M.I.T. Corporation could no longer continue to manage the Instrumentation Laboratory.[2] His announcement followed a year-long controversy over military-related research on campus, a con-

[1] "Statement of President Howard W. Johnson," in M.I.T., *Institute Report*, November 3, 1969.

[2] In January 1970, the laboratory's name was changed to the Charles Stark Draper Laboratory. Since most of the events in this study occurred when it was still called the Instrumentation Laboratory, I will use the former name.

troversy that had as its prime target this laboratory, well known for the design and development of inertial guidance systems. The Instrumentation Laboratory was a major resource at M.I.T., receiving $54.6 million from the Department of Defense (DOD) and National Aeronautics and Space Administration (NASA) for mission-oriented projects in 1969. For M.I.T., these projects were a rewarding source of prestige, educational opportunity, and research funding, providing one-quarter of the total operating budget of the university. M.I.T.'s position as a leading technical university had developed largely through such work on advanced technology supported by the government, and its commitments to faculty and long-term professional employees required continued dependence on government sponsors. But government sponsorship was also a burden; the size and the character of Instrumentation Laboratory projects and the location of a development facility right on campus were highly controversial.

The events at M.I.T. that led to the decision to divest the Instrumentation Laboratory brought forth some significant issues concerning science and its relationship to society. To what extent are scientists and technologists responsible for the use and misuse of their work? How can well-developed technical resources be reallocated to cope with contemporary social problems? Related to these general questions were those that concerned the relationship of the university to national priorities. What criteria should be used to establish university research policy? Is the university a neutral organization or does involvement in military research define the university as a political institution?

The ties between universities and the defense establishment developed following World War II, as agencies with military-related interests became the major source of support for advanced technical research and development. These ties, later nurtured by the concern with Soviet expansionism and technological advance, were mutually rewarding. In the context of the times, university scientists supported "wholehearted collaboration"[3] with military objectives, a collaboration that was crucial to the development of the nation's scientific capabilities and institutions. But the price was high; increasingly relationships with government agencies created a dilemma for universities,[4] for their responsibilities, beyond teaching and research, are ill defined. The desirable balance between public service and academic research, the appropriate character of activities linked with outside groups, and the institutional forms through which these activities are organized are contentious questions related to a more general concern about the scientist's

[3] From the report of the Riehlman Committee on the position of scientists in the government service. Reviewed by Edward Shils in *Science and Freedom*, November 1954 to August 1956, p. 23.

[4] See Jack Ruina, "The University-Managed Laboratory," in Bruce Smith and D. C. Hague (eds.), *The Dilemma of Accountability in Modern Government: Independence Versus Control* (London: MacMillan, 1971).

participation in research related to military development and about his responsibility for the use of his work.[5]

The idea that scientists have a particular obligation of "responsibility" for the use of their work developed during the postwar period and has since been an important part of the scientific ethic. Scientists became involved as experts in government service and, also, as critics. Concerned about the increasing development of nuclear weapons, they attempted to influence state policy.[6] As a group, however, scientists have generally approached political issues with reluctance,[7] making a clear distinction between their responsibility as researchers and their desire to have an influence on political issues. As Robert Wood has noted, the influence of scientists "does not come about by conscious adaptation to the political world. . . . The group is an apolitical elite, triumphing in the political arena to the extent to which it disavows political objectives and refuses to

[5] Harvey Brooks notes that service to the state has often been a "serious problem of conscience for the more thoughtful members of the scientific community." See "Impact of the Defense Establishment on Science and Education," *National Science Policy*, in U.S. House of Representatives, Subcommittee on Science, Research and Development of the Committee on Science and Astronautics, *Hearings*, 91st Congress, 2nd session, October 1970, p. 932.

[6] Robert Gilpin, *American Scientists and Nuclear Weapons Policy* (Princeton: Princeton University Press, 1962), p. 23.

[7] Joseph Haberer, *Politics and the Community of Science* (New York: Van Nostrand Reinhold, 1969), p. 1. See also Richard A. Rettig, "Science, Technology, and Public Policy," *World Politics*, 23 (January 1971), 273 ff.

behave according to conventional political practice." [8]

The validity of an apolitical ethic has become questionable, as the consequences of the use of scientific research in advanced military technology have blurred the traditional line between the practice of science and its application. Moreover, the high cost of research alone suggests that scientific activity must be closely articulated with political decisions about technical applications. Jean Salomon has described the scientist's situation as "circumscribed in a framework of political decisions which affect his research work and which his work affects. . . . Science, conceived as a discourse of truth, can no longer be disassociated from the function it fills. Its value is based largely on its promise of application." [9]

Past efforts of members of the scientific community to influence government decisions had taken several forms. Dissenting positions on controversial issues appeared in journals (e.g., *Bulletin of the Atomic Scientists*, *Science*) and were embodied in organizations (e.g., the Federation of American Scientists (FAS) and Scientists' Institute for Public Information (SIPI)). Some individuals refused to work in certain scientific areas. In 1946, for example, Norbert Wiener, then at M.I.T., published a dramatic letter in which he declared "that to provide scientific information is not necessarily an innocent act. I do not

[8] Robert C. Wood, "Scientists and Politics: The Rise of an Apolitical Elite," in Robert Gilpin and Christopher Wright (eds.), *Scientists and Rational Policy Making* (New York: Columbia University Press, 1964), p. 44.

[9] Jean Salomon, "The Internationale of Science," *Science Studies*, 1 (January 1971), 23, 40.

expect to publish any future work of mine which may do damage in the hands of irresponsible militarists." [10]

While organizations such as the FAS engaged in part-time lobbying, rarely did scientists try to organize the scientific community as a group for protest or political action.[11] Several exceptions served as precedents for the events at M.I.T. In 1946, the pacifist A. J. Muste called on leading scientists to refuse to work on atomic weapons. This evoked uneasy response from the chairman of the Federation of American Scientists: "If scientists were to walk out on all military projects they would be taking the law into their own hands just as surely as the Ku Klux Klan." A strike, according to Hans Bethe, "would only antagonize the public of the United States who would rightly accuse us of trying to dictate the policies of the country." [12]

A call for a work stoppage in 1954 to protest the government's handling of the Oppenheimer case and to call for a review of the security system was criticized as a "rash action" by the scientific establishment. "There should be complete removal of the system from politics,"

[10] Norbert Wiener, "A Scientist Rebels," *Atlantic Monthly*, 179 (January 1947), 46.

[11] Gilpin, *op. cit.*, extensively discusses the postwar role of scientists with respect to government nuclear weapons policy. See also Lawrence S. Wittner, *Rebels against War* (New York: Columbia University Press, 1969), pp. 200, 241. Criticism, however, has almost entirely been focused on this issue. Until recently, scientists have avoided taking leadership roles in issues relating to the use of technology, the most striking case in point being the initial response to Rachel Carson's *Silent Spring*.

[12] Quoted in Wittner, *op. cit.*, p. 176.

said Vannevar Bush. "There will be no scientific strike."[13]

In the political context of the late 1960's, "problems of conscience" in the scientific community led to serious disenchantment with the symbiotic relationship between science and the government. Scientific radicalism as expressed at M.I.T. during 1969–1970 developed out of the postwar "ethic of responsibility," and, indeed, many of the participants in the events at M.I.T. had earlier contributed their expertise to issues such as arms control. But the M.I.T. events differed; first, in the use of overtly political tactics and, second, in the attempt to bring about an institutional action that would effect a change in government policy. The change in tactics apparent at M.I.T. and other universities in the late 1960's[14] is also suggested by the willingness of many scientists to express their individual commitments in the form of organized political action. When the Harvard geneticist James Shapiro abandoned his career for full-time political activity in late 1969,[15] he intended to organize scientists to work actively for radical political change. Many recent

[13] Vannevar Bush, quoted in Irwin Goodwin, "The AAAS at Berkeley," *Bulletin of the Atomic Scientists,* 11 (March 1955), 84.

[14] In April 1968, the Columbia University affiliation with the Institute for Defense Analysis was an important focus of the student uprising. The Cornell Aeronautical Laboratory, the Stanford Research Center, and other university laboratories have also been subject to protest (see Table 4, p. 28). The tragic results of the bombing of the Mathematics Center at the University of Wisconsin in August 1970, however, turned many activists away from this issue.

[15] *Nature,* 224 (December 27, 1969).

petitions and publications have aimed at mustering the potential strength of an organized scientific community to influence policy. As a part of the ABM controversy, for example, two hundred physicists demonstrated at the White House and presented a petition with 1,100 signatures to the President. In June 1970, 44 Nobel Laureates drafted an appeal to Nixon publicly declaring their opposition to the war in Southeast Asia, and 200 industrial scientists went to Washington to lobby for cutting off military funds for further operations in Vietnam.[16] In November of the same year, 750 scientists signed a petition urging the Senate to kill a proposal for defense facilities and industrial security that they viewed as threatening to personal liberties.

Activist organizations and publications have proliferated. SIPI has grown into a substantial organization providing leadership for environmental groups, and the Federation of American Scientists has hired a full-time professional lobbyist. The circulation of *Science*, the journal of the AAAS, grew from 31,504 in 1954 to 146,898 in 1968, and its former well-known political reporter, Daniel Greenberg, has started a new weekly newsletter devoted specifically to the politics of science.[17]

More dramatic activity began with the organization at Stanford of SESPA (Scientists and Engineers for Social and Political Action), which now has a membership of

---

[16] *Science*, 168 (June 12, 1970), 1325.
[17] *Science and Government Report* began publication in February 1971.

about 3,000. Created in February 1969 as a radical caucus within the American Physical Society (APS), its formation coincided with the movement at M.I.T. and helped to make the work stoppage that precipitated the Instrumentation Laboratory controversy a multi-university activity. SESPA was instrumental in drafting a petition signed by five hundred members of the APS requesting a new division for discussing political issues. Its success was significant in light of the reluctance of professional scientific societies to be involved in politics.[18] In addition, SESPA is willing to employ overtly political tactics. Seeking open recognition of the political role of scientists, SESPA uses tactics directed not only to influencing governmental decisions, but to forcing change through organized and, if necessary, rebellious action. SESPA is more like a trade union than a professional association.

Similarly, an "adversary system of scientific inquiry" has been reflected in the formation of public interest organizations such as the Center for Science in the Public Interest, a "spin-off" from Ralph Nader's Center for Study of Responsive Law.[19] Many scientists and technologists remain hostile toward such organizations. Regarding their "responsibility" as extending only to the quality of their work, they see the use or misuse of that work as a question in another domain. Others, whose

[18] *The Tech,* February 18, 1969.

[19] *Science,* 173 (July 9, 1971), 131. See John W. Gofman and Arthur R. Tamplin, "Toward an Adversary System of Scientific Inquiry," *Poisoned Power, The Case against Nuclear Power Plants* (Emmaus, Pa.: Rodale Press, 1971), ch. 12.

convictions have brought them into politics, are often repelled by overtly political procedures.[20] Although they often support the philosophical position of activists concerning research priorities, the dilemma of "social responsibility," the conflict between the dictates of individual conscience and the institutional interests supported by existing priorities, leads to ambivalence. This dilemma, we shall see, determined the shape of moral politics and its consequences at M.I.T. as activists hoped, by political means, to force an institutional response to an "ethic of responsibility." [21]

There had been relatively little political activity at the Institute before 1969, although the pervasive restlessness brought about by the Vietnam war had been expressed sporadically during 1967 and 1968 in events related to draft resistance and job recruitment for defense industries. Then, on March 4, 1969, a group of M.I.T. students and faculty initiated a national "research stoppage" to call attention to what they considered the mis-

[20] Gilpin, *op. cit.*, p. 304. Warner Schilling, in Robert Gilpin and Christopher Wright (eds.), *Scientists and National Policy Making* (New York: Columbia University Press, 1964), has noted: "The scientific expert . . . has no real hope of keeping out of politics; his only choice is in the character of his political style" (p. 164).

[21] Max Weber distinguished the "ethic of responsibility" from the "ethic of ultimate ends" and noted the paradox that those who follow the ethic of responsibility and engage in politics must often engage in violent means to achieve good ends. Max Weber, *Politics as a Vocation* (1919), H. H. Gerth and C. Wright Mills, translators (Philadelphia: Fortress Press, 1965), pp. 46–53.

use of scientific and technical resources. Pressing the
issue that easily funded military projects were influencing the direction of research, the activists demanded the
conversion of university technological resources to social
objectives.

This direct action set in motion a process of political
negotiation between the activists and the administration
that centered on the use of the resources of the Instrumentation Laboratory. The activists' demands, however,
threatened interests and careers that had become well
established by years of government-sponsored research.
M.I.T., like other universities, was experiencing financial
difficulties and had to consider the consequences of
losing government sponsorship. While the administration
shared the activists' concern with the direction of research at the Instrumentation Laboratory and its appropriateness at M.I.T., they had difficulty dealing with the
demands to reallocate laboratory resources, a difficulty
suggesting the institutional inertia that obstructs attempts to change existing priorities.

The M.I.T. decision to divest the laboratory took
place in a context defined by economic and political
circumstances and by the conflicting concerns of laboratory employees, students, faculty, and government sponsors.[22] Their diverse interests were revealed when moral

[22] The analysis assumes that decisions are made in a context
of relationships among actors, conditions, and events. A model
for this assumption is developed in Richard C. Snyder, H. W.
Bruck, and Burton Sapin, *Foreign Policy and Decision Making*
(New York: The Free Press, 1962), pp. 81–82. See also John J.

politics threatened disruption. The dynamics of the events of 1969 suggest the complex of irreconcilable interests and conflicting concepts of public responsibility and individual rights that are brought to bear on institutional decisions. With the announcement that the Instrumentation Laboratory would be divested from the Institute, a sense of relief pervaded the campus, for the decision averted an immediate crisis. But the decision was unpalatable both for those committed to retaining the existing relationship as well as for those who had worked for conversion of the laboratories' resources in the hope that such dramatic action would influence national policy. Moreover, for M.I.T. to immediately sever the laboratory would pose a financial dilemma that left considerable ambiguity concerning the terms of divestment and the significance of the decision itself.

The following case study of how a major technical institution dealt with a challenge concerning the direction and control of its technological resources sheds light on several issues: the complexities involved in the relationship between government sponsorship and university research, the problems of defining appropriate research and public service policy in universities, and the institutional constraints placed upon attempts to bring moral considerations of "social responsibility" to

---

Corson, "Machinery Needed to Harmonize Technological Development and Social Policy," in James C. Charlesworth (ed.), *Harmonizing Technological Development and Social Policy in America* (American Academy of Political and Social Science Monograph 11; Philadelphia, December 1970), p. 220.

bear on scientific and technological research. Before examining the events of 1969, I will describe the particular context at M.I.T. in which these events took place.

I / The Massachusetts Institute of Technology

When M.I.T.'s first building was inaugurated in 1865, the local press celebrated the new institute as "the tomb of dead languages." For instead of classical studies "whose general pursuit is of no further earthly use to anyone alive," [1] the purpose of this institute, as stated in its charter, was to aid in "the advancement, development and practical applications of science in connection with the arts, culture, manufacture, and commerce." [2] A course of studies was offered "for students seeking to qualify themselves for the professions of the Mechanical Engineer, Civil Engineer, Practical Chemist, Engineer of Mines, and of Builder and Architect." [3]

Since that time, M.I.T. has developed, especially in

[1] Quoted from an article in *Frank Leslie's Illustrated Newspaper*, December 17, 1869, in Karl T. Compton, *Massachusetts Institute of Technology*, Address to the Newcomen Society of England (New York, 1948).

[2] Compton, *op. cit.*, p. 24.

[3] From the first catalogue of 1865, quoted in Samuel C. Prescott, *When M.I.T. Was Boston Tech.*, (Cambridge: The Technology Press, 1954), p. 51.

the last ten years, from a technical institution to a university, dominated by scientists and including social scientists and humanists. Its initial enrollment of fifteen students and an operating budget of $30,000 has grown to over 7,000 students and a budget exceeding $200 million. Its growth has mirrored the dramatically changing pattern of scientific and technological development in the United States since World War II.

The climate in which M.I.T. developed its ties to government agencies was established during that war, when the Institute participated as the largest university contracting for defense research and development and as a major source of top scientific advisers for the armed forces. All four non-military personnel on the governing body of the National Defense Research Committee of the Office of Scientific Research and Development were from M.I.T.[4] Wartime relationships between the military and scientists led to "toleration, if not support, of the military establishment, . . . and a climate of intellectual opinion which made cooperation with the military establishment more comfortable than normal in American History."[5]

The recognition of scientific research and develop-

---

[4] For a discussion of M.I.T.'s role during the war, see John Burchard, *M.I.T. in World War II, Q.E.D.* (New York: John Wiley, 1948).

[5] Harvey Brooks, "Impact of the Defense Establishment on Science and Education," *National Science Policy*, in U.S. House of Representatives, Subcommittee on Science, Research and Development of the Committee on Science and Astronautics, *Hearings*, 91st Congress, 2nd session, October 1970, p. 942.

ment as a crucial aspect of diplomacy and military force resulted in a postwar system of federal support of science through grants and contracts. As scientific research became a national objective, the Institute became a major recipient of funds. Before the war, 58 per cent of the M.I.T. operating budget was derived from student fees, 35 per cent from investment, and only 7 per cent from other sources.[6] By 1940, defense research contracts alone already totaled more than the entire 1939 budget; and when M.I.T. was fully mobilized in 1944, the annual budget reached $44,354,800. The pattern established during this period shaped the future of M.I.T.

In 1947, James Killian, then M.I.T. vice-president and later its president, noted:

The concentration of war research on its campus, the presence here of a great assemblage of gifted scientists from hundreds of institutions and the remarkably varied activities of its own staff . . . contributed in one overwhelming way to the establishment of a fresh and vigorous post-war program. I refer to the wholesale cross-fertilization that resulted; no one at M.I.T. during this period can fail to be impressed by the ferment of ideas, the prevailing temper to re-evaluate and strike out in new directions, and the broadened concept of the Institute's responsibilities.[7]

Wartime activities made M.I.T. a center for "big science," large-scale, usually applied research relating to

[6] Burchard, *op. cit.*, p. 4. A general discussion of the pattern of support of science appears in Vannevar Bush, *Pieces of the Action* (New York: William Morrow, 1970), pp. 63–65.

[7] James R. Killian, Jr., "M.I.T. Redeploys for Peace," in Burchard, *op. cit.*, pp. 314–315.

the technical needs of the government.[8] Federally sponsored research grew astronomically and the proportion
of graduate students and faculty increased (see Table 1).
This increase in sponsored research was closely associated
with the rapidly developing importance of federally
supported laboratories in which work was integrated with

Table 1. Enrollment, faculty, and sponsored research at M.I.T.,
1938–1970 *

Year	Total students	Under-grads	Grads	Faculty	Total staff	Sponsored research
1938–39	3093	2401	692	282	683	$ 18,923
1939–40	3100	2379	721	285	681	1,296,000
1944–45	1198	849	349	330	582	44,354,800
1946–47	5172	3811	1361	398	1244	9,825,000
1956–57	6000	3688	2312	607	1856	49,118,000
1959–60	6270	3580	2690	670	2148	66,550,000
1961–62	6454	3562	2892	773	2441	91,093,724
1962–63	6695	3553	3142	794	2642	113,634,614
1964–65	7151	3640	3511	841	2723	140,424,644
1965–66	7408	3690	3718	905	2808	148,174,383
1968–69	7764	3955	3809	900	3024	176,206,294
1969–70	8024	4074	3950	1050	3300	171,294,000

* M.I.T., *Report of the President* and *Report of the Registrar*
(Cambridge, for the years listed).

national policy. By 1969, of about 100 labs at M.I.T.,
the two largest were Lincoln Laboratory and the Instrumentation Laboratory (I-Lab); combined, they ac-
counted for 51 per cent of the university's total budget
of $217,505,000.[9]

[8] Alvin M. Weinberg, *Reflections on Big Science* (Cambridge:
The M.I.T. Press, 1967).
[9] This budget is handled as a partnership arrangement between four segments of the Corporation, each of which re-
imburses the Institute for costs in relation to its percentage of

The Instrumentation Laboratory's 1969 budget of $54.6 million came entirely from agencies supporting mission-oriented projects, primarily from the National Aeronautics and Space Agency (NASA) and the Department of Defense (DOD) (see Table 3). The Lincoln Laboratory budget was $66,833,000—higher than that of all on-campus research. As a Federal Contract Research Center (FCRC), Lincoln Laboratory received its core funding on a fixed annual basis as a single contract from the Department of Defense. On-campus research funds ($58,800,000 in 1969) came from a number of sources, primarily from the federal government, but only about 27 per cent, or $16,900,000, came from the DOD.[10] On-campus contracts, concentrated in academic engineering, were all nonclassified.

---

the whole. Percentages, somewhat confusing due to overlapping categories, are calculated by the comptroller as follows: Instrumentation Lab, 24 per cent; Lincoln Lab, 27 per cent; on-campus research, 30 per cent; and instructional groups, 19 per cent. Letter from Paul V. Cusick, comptroller, to Dr. Albert G. Hill, vice president for research at M.I.T., 1969.

[10] These figures are based on the M.I.T. comptroller's reports and include only on-campus research funds. The term "on-campus" has no geographic implications but refers to research directly tied to academic departments. This excludes the Special Laboratories. Other sources of funding are as follows: $8.6 million from the AEC, $8.1 million from NIH, $6.5 million from NASA, $6.4 million from NSF, $3.6 million from other federal agencies, and $8 million from private sources. According to NSF listings of all federal obligations to universities, the DOD contributes about 41 per cent of the funds received by M.I.T. from federal agencies. In contrast, the DOD contributed 8.07 per cent of the total federal obligation to all universities and colleges in 1969.

Together, Lincoln Laboratory and the Instrumentation Laboratory have made M.I.T. a major contractor for DOD research. In 1968, the Institute ranked fifty-fourth in a list of 100 organizations receiving the largest dollar value of military prime contracts, and it was the only university on this list. It also ranked tenth in a list of prime contractors for research, development, test, and evaluation work, and was the first university on this list.[11] A popular view of the relationship between M.I.T. and the federal government was dramatically summarized in 1966 by an attorney representing M.I.T.'s interests concerning the routing of a proposed highway.

M.I.T. is in the front rank of the forces of Science dedicated to the essential research which the Government of the United States considers indispensable to the National Defense. It is a scientific arsenal of democracy. From its halls and laboratories come the knowledge and technique, the brain power and the resources which contribute to our national survival in an era where the laboratories and technicians of our enemies work sleeplessly to outdistance us in the race to harness the latent secrets of nature as tools of their supremacy.[12]

[11] DOD, Directorate for Statistical Services, 1968. Data on government spending for research depend on what commitments are included in the budget estimates. Federal Contract Research Centers, for example, are included in DOD listings but not in NSF listings.

[12] Edward B. Hanify, at a public hearing, as reported in the Boston *Herald Traveler*, February 21, 1966. The proposed routing of the inner belt highway would have affected the Instrumentation Laboratory.

The size of its external commitments has had several implications for M.I.T. First, reimbursement for overhead serves as an important source of funds for ongoing expenses such as heat, maintenance, and administrative costs.[13] It allows the university to distribute the cost of such items and thus frees resources that can be used for academic purposes. Reimbursement to M.I.T. from both Special Laboratories since World War II totaled $237,000,000. Second, these external commitments affect the educational process; the favorable teacher-student ratio at M.I.T. is at least in part due to the increased cash flow brought in by the Special Labs. In addition, the research interests of the faculty feed into the university classroom and laboratory. According to Seymour Melman, a critic of university-military relationships, "Options that always exist in fields of engineering technology are informed by the extramural activities of the faculty." [14]

As one of the leading technical institutions in the world, M.I.T.'s faculty has been actively involved with those agencies dealing with high priority national scientific and technological problems. In particular, there are numerous links between the M.I.T. faculty and the DOD reflecting the major role of the DOD in advanced technical development. Jack Ruina, a long-time member of the

[13] Calculated at 46 per cent of salaries and wages as of May 1969, overhead pays for indirect expenses such as administration, library, and various services.

[14] Seymour Melman, *Pentagon Capitalism* (New York: McGraw-Hill, 1970), p. 101.

M.I.T. faculty and vice president for the Special Laboratories, had been assistant director of Defense Research and Engineering and director of the Advanced Research Project Agency of the DOD. Members of the faculty sit on air force, army, and navy scientific advisory boards and consult for the Pentagon and for military contractors.[15] Of the 75 largest Pentagon contractors in 1968, 19 were represented in the M.I.T. Corporation, including Lockheed, the main contractor for Poseidon.

Striking changes in the direction of technical education coincided with the growth of big science at M.I.T. and other universities. The Institute assumed leadership in a national trend in engineering education that emphasized mathematics and basic science. This change in perspective was also evident in the increased student choice of science over engineering beginning in the late 1950's. In 1958, 67 per cent of the entering students had stated their preference for engineering and 22 per cent for science. Ten years later only 31 per cent of the entering students preferred engineering and 52 per cent preferred science, a change that in 1969 led the dean of engineering to conclude that "science has displaced en-

[15] Among those faculty who sat on Pentagon advisory boards in 1969 were: Professors Ithiel Da Sola Pool, Department of Political Science; René H. Miller, Department of Aeronautics and Astronautics; Edward B. Roberts, School of Management; Holt Ashley, Department of Aeronautical Engineering; Charles S. Draper, Instrumentation Laboratory; Frank E. Heart, Lincoln Laboratory; Winston R. Markey, Experimental Astronomy Laboratory.

gineering as a dominant interest of freshmen at M.I.T." [16]

There was also significant change in the distribution of students in the various schools at M.I.T., with an especially large increase in the humanities in 1968 (see Table 2). New schools and departments were established during this period, including the School of Humanities and Social Sciences in 1950, the Sloan School of Industrial

Table 2. Distribution of students at M.I.T., 1955–1969

Year	Architecture & planning	Engineering	Humanities & social science (estab. 1950)	Industrial management (Sloan School, estab. 1952)	Science	Undesignated first year	Total
955–56 *	147	2327	28	313	666		5348
959–60	194	3008	219	384	1529	936	6270
961–62	190	2936	267	399	1669	993	6454
964–65	200	3065	358	437	1845	1246	7151
968–69	295	3192	621	499	2013	1144	7764

Sources: All figures are from M.I.T., Report of the President (Cambridge, for he years listed, unless otherwise noted).
* "U.S. Colleges: Tabular Data," The College Bluebook (New York, C.C.M. nformation Corporation).

Management in 1952, the Department of Psychology in 1963, and the Department of Political Science in 1965. As M.I.T. clearly evolved from a technical institute to a full-scale university, there were inevitable changes in the student orientation to political issues. Furthermore, change in the concept of education produced consider-

[16] Raymond Bisplinghoff, "Report of the Dean," M.I.T. Bulletin, 1968–69, p. 50.

able internal strain. In 1964, for example, President Julius A. Stratton noted:

On the one extreme is a view that the undergraduate experience should focus on mathematics, basic science, and the humanities; and in engineering, upon broad and fundamental areas . . . cutting across all the fields of applied science. A substantial number of our engineering faculty, on the other hand, are convinced that such a move would spell the end of engineering education as we have known it at M.I.T.[17]

These academic changes on the one hand, combined with big science and government-supported, mission-oriented projects on the other, also left considerable uncertainty about the basic nature of the Institute. "Some observers claim it is difficult . . . to tell whether Massachusetts Institute of Technology is a university with many government research institutions appended to it or a cluster of government research laboratories with a very good educational institution attached to it." [18]

[17] Julius A. Stratton, "To the Corporation," in M.I.T., *Report of the President* (Cambridge, 1964), pp. 40–41.

[18] Alvin M. Weinberg, "The Federal Laboratories and Science Education," *Science*, 136 (April 16, 1962), 30.

II / Ménage à Trois:
The University, Federal
Support, and the
Instrumentation Laboratory

Universities and Federal Laboratories

American universities have been profoundly affected by the system of federal funding of research and development that provides at least 20 per cent of their operating revenue.[1] In 1969, federal obligations for the 100 universities and colleges receiving the most support totaled $2,387,262,000. M.I.T. was first in this group, receiving 4.10 per cent of the total government spending on academic science. Table 3 lists the major sources of

[1] In 1966–1967 this funding totaled $1.3 billion. Federal funds tend to be concentrated in those universities with the largest Ph.D. output and graduate enrollment. In 1967, 16 universities received 38 per cent of all federal R&D funds directed to universities. The top 100 recipients of federal obligations received 88 per cent of all federal R&D funds. This funding also tends to be proportional to institutional expenditures and to the size of the graduate program. National Science Foundation, *Federal Support to Universities and Colleges 1967* (Washington, D.C.: GPO, 1969).

funding for the ten universities receiving the most funding.

Universities make various arrangements to administer their federally sponsored projects. Laboratories receiving federal funds vary considerably both in size and in their relationship to the sponsoring agency and parent university.[2] One type of laboratory is the Federal Contract Research Center, funded primarily by a single federal agency.[3] Eighteen such laboratories, including M.I.T.'s Lincoln Laboratory, are associated with universities. Listed as a line item in the federal budget, the FCRC's receive a core of stable funding from year to year and do not depend on competition for mission-oriented contracts. The funding comes from the AEC, NASA, or the DOD, and often, according to the NSF, "their creation and operation are not primarily related to the main function of the administering universities."[4]

---

[2] In a study of the variation in relationships, Jack Ruina distinguishes between off-campus university-managed laboratories, university-affiliated (but not university-managed) laboratories, and on-campus labs that are in the mainstream of academic activities. Jack Ruina, "The University Managed Laboratory," in Bruce Smith and D. C. Hague (eds.), *The Dilemma of Accountability in Modern Government: Independence versus Control* (London: MacMillan, 1971), pp. 118–128.

[3] These are also called Federally Funded Research and Development Centers (FFRDC). Dean C. Coddington and J. Gordon Milliken, "Future of Federal Contract Research Centers," *Harvard Business Review*, 48 (March–April 1970), 103–116.

[4] National Science Foundation, *op. cit.*, p. 45.

Table 3. Federal obligations to universities, 1969 (in thousands) *

| University | Total | Major Contributing Agencies | | | | | |
		AEC	DOD	HEW	NASA	NSF	Other
M.I.T.	$97,604	$9,568	$40,274 †	$12,066	$27,468	$ 7,553	$ 657
Harvard	69,558	2,494	3,038	44,490	10,357	7,284	1,895
U. of Mich.	61,448	3,101	11,317	34,281	3,176	6,769	2,804
U. of Wash.	56,398	2,685	2,647	42,625	629	6,539	1,273
U.C.L.A.	53,129	4,761	2,039	36,172	5,444	4,091	622
Columbia	52,375	4,894	6,347	34,055	958	5,526	595
U. of Wisc.	51,748	3,368	1,064	31,564	1,797	7,251	6,704
Stanford	51,593	715	10,359	24,100	5,032	10,797	590
Berkeley	50,689	729	4,358	22,354	5,988	11,141	6,119
U. of Minn.	50,102	1,832	2,916	33,815	2,367	3,901	5,271

* National Science Foundation, *Federal Support to Universities, Colleges, and Selected Nonprofit Institutions, Fiscal Year 1969*, NSF 70–27 (Washington, D.C.: GPO), p. 16.

† Note that this is not consistent with the on-campus research funds as computed by the university comptroller. NSF listings include funds for research and development, for research and development plant, and for other science and non-science activities. They exclude Lincoln Laboratory.

Other university-managed laboratories work on research contracts (see Table 4). Some are on-campus laboratories closely integrated with academic research and teaching. Others are similar to the FCRC's in that they are off-campus and engage in the development of military and space systems, but they are usually funded on the basis of proposals for particular missions. Their work ranges from basic research to advanced engineering development of hardware systems; those engaged in the latter often closely cooperate with government personnel and industrial contractors and are comparatively independent of their parent universities. The Instrumentation Lab is of this type.

Table 4. Federally supported university-managed laboratories in the United States, 1969–1970

University	Laboratory	Major sponsoring agency	Funding (in millions of dollars)	Number of employees	Remarks
		A. Federal Contract Research Centers			
American University *	Center for Research in Social Systems	DOD (Army)	i-1.8	62/81	Separated from American University in December 1969, now affiliated with American Institute for Research.
California Institute of Technology (CIT) *	Jet Propulsion Laboratory	NASA	i-54.3 ex-42.3	1917/3640	
University of California (Berkeley) †	Lawrence Radiation Laboratory	AEC	37.7	3465	
University of California †	Naval Biological Laboratory	DOD (Navy)	2.0	148	
Columbia †	Hudson Laboratories	DOD (Navy)	4.7	381	Has been closed. Functions merged with Naval Research Laboratory (an in-house Navy lab)
George Washing-	Human Resources Re-	DOD (Army)	3.4	264	October 1969, be-

Table 4. (*continued*)

University	Laboratory	A. Federal Contract Research Centers			Remarks
		Major sponsoring agency	*Funding (in millions of dollars)*	*Number of employees*	
ton University †	search Office				came a nonprofit, independent corporation.
Iowa State University of Science and Technology †	Ames Laboratory	AEC	8.3	1012	
Johns Hopkins *	Applied Physics Laboratory	DOD (Navy)	i-34.1 ex-12.1	1088/1300	
MIT †	Francis Bitter National Magnet Laboratory	DOD (Air Force)	2.5	109	
MIT *	Lincoln Laboratory	DOD (Air Force)	i-40. ex-27.5	612/1141	
MIT and Harvard †	Cambridge Electron Accelator	AEC	3.6	193	
Pennsylvania State *	Ordnance Research Laboratory	DOD (Navy)	i-7.4 ex-1.1	185/263	
Princeton †	Princeton Plasma Physics Laboratory	AEC	6.3	423	
Princeton and University of Pennsylvania †	Princeton-Penn Accelator	AEC	5.1	315	
University of Rochester †	Center for Naval Analyses	DOD (Navy)	9.3	450	

Table 4. (*continued*)

A. Federal Contract Research Centers

University	Laboratory	Major sponsoring agency	Funding (in millions of dollars)	Number of employees	Remarks
Stanford †	Stanford Linear Accelator Center	AEC	22.4	1228	
University of Washington †	Applied Physics Laboratory	DOD (Navy)	2.9	170	
William and Mary *	Space Radiation Effects Laboratory	NASA	i-1.3 ex- .99	6/52	

B. Other federally supported laboratories

University	Laboratory	Major sponsoring agency	Funding	Number of employees	Remarks
University of Alaska *	Arctic Research Laboratory	DOD (Navy)	i-1.5 million	30/110	
CIT *	Jet Propulsion Laboratory, Deep Space Network	NASA	i-32,079,000 ex-17,615,000	608/828	
CIT *	Jet Propulsion Laboratory, Edwards Test Station	NASA	i-1,900,000	18/65	
CIT *	Jet Propulsion Laboratory, Table Mountain Facility	NASA	i-500,000	2/3	

Table 4. *(continued)*

B. Other federally supported laboratories

University	Laboratory	Major sponsoring agency	Funding	Number of employees	Remarks
Cornell §	Arecibo	DOD (Air Force)	i-1.8 million	23/224	Sale of CAL to EDP announced in September 1968, but blocked. Supreme Court injunction presently being appealed.
	Cornell Aeronautical Laboratory		ex-17.1 million, 1967	800	
Illinois Institute of Technology §	Research Institute	DOD	13.5 million		
University of Michigan	Willow Run	DOD	11 million	270/330	
MIT §	Instrumentation Laboratory	DOD and NASA	20 million	2,000	May 1970 administration announced decision to divest laboratory
MIT *	Bedford Research Facility	NASA	i-200,000 ex- 20,000	7/11	
Ohio State University §	Defense Management Center	DOD (Air Force)	1.2 million	50	
Stanford §	Stanford Research Institute	DOD	30.6 million	2200	Sold to Institute's Board for $25 million January 1970

Table 4. (continued)

B. Other federally supported laboratories

University	Laboratory	Major sponsoring agency	Funding	Number of employees	Remarks
Stanford §	Electronics Laboratory		Over 1 million in classified contracts in 1969		May 1969, administration agreed to terminate all classified contracts
University of Syracuse §	Research Corporation		4 million	350	
University of Texas §	Defense Research Laboratory		3 million		
Tufts §	Human Engineering and Analysis Service	DOD (Army)			

i = intramural   ex = extramural

Where only one figure is given in employee column it is the number of total staff. Where two are given, the first is the number of R&D professionals and the second is total staff.

* *Directory of Federal R&D Installations* for the year ending June 30, 1969. A report to the Federal Council for Science and Technology. National Science Foundation 70-23.

† Dean C. Coddington and J. Gordon Milliken, "Future of Federal Contract Research Centers," *Harvard Business Review*, 48 (March–April 1970), 103–116.

§ *The University-Military-Police Complex: A Directory and Related Documents*, compiled by Michael Klare (New York: The North American Congress on Latin America, 1970).

There are numerous advantages for the government in working with major universities. Salaries and overhead costs are often lower than in industry, and competent staff is readily available, attracted by the university affiliation. For the universities, there are also advantages:

increased expertise, consulting opportunities for faculty, and "real world" professional engineering facilities for students. But the costs are high. Some of the arguments concerning the consequences of postwar involvement with the government have been outlined by Harvey Brooks, dean of engineering and applied science at Harvard.[5] One major concern is that the military has undue influence on the character of research, and that this influence leads to overspecialization in those technical fields of interest to the military and to the neglect of other fields.[6] Also, the availability of external support has been blamed for an alleged emphasis on research at the expense of teaching and for weakening the institutional commitment of faculty.[7] Furthermore, it is argued, military support erodes the independence of the university and inhibits criticism of government policy.

Those who support the pattern of military sponsorship claim, on the other hand, that it has in fact provided broad and flexible support, stimulating development in many areas of basic research and encouraging new experi-

[5] Harvey Brooks, "Impact of the Defense Establishment on Science and Education," *National Science Policy,* in U.S. House of Representatives, Subcommittee on Science, Research & Development of the Committee on Science and Astronautics, *Hearings,* 91st Congress, 2nd Session, October 1970.

[6] See also U.S. House of Representatives, Committee on Government Operations, *Conflicts Between the Federal Research Programs and the Nation's Goals for Higher Education,* Report, 89th Congress, 1st session (Washington, D.C.: GPO, 1965).

[7] Julius A. Stratton, "To the Corporation," in M.I.T., *Report of the President* (Cambridge, 1963), p. 39.

mental techniques that have accelerated advance in many divergent fields. They argue that the mechanism of sponsorship has not made as much of a difference in institutional priorities as is popularly believed; in any case, these priorities are determined by academic scientists who evaluate proposals. In reviewing the consequences of university-government relationships, Harvey Brooks cites evidence that research-oriented faculty do in fact devote more time to teaching than to research and that government-supported scientists have not hesitated to criticize government policy, though there are well known cases in which scientists, critical of national policy, have lost funding.[8]

The problematic implications of government involvement have long been apparent, but in the immediate postwar years, when national foreign policy was far more widely accepted than it is today, the costs of involvement were also more acceptable. When national policy becomes controversial, however, this is reflected in the reevaluation of the costs and benefits of military sponsorship of research.

Federal laboratories have been a particular source of strain on university campuses because they are responsible primarily to their government sponsors and highly independent of university administration. They have, for example, been able to carry on classified research at a

[8] Contrast Brooks, *op. cit.*, with Serge Lang, "The DOD, Government and Universities," in Martin Brown (ed.), *The Social Responsibility of the Scientist* (New York: Free Press, 1971).

time when such projects are prohibited on most campuses. Also, many federal labs operate in the style of
industrial laboratories, seeing their projects through to
production. Finally, the substance of their research, often
directly associated with weapons development, has been
the focus of heated controversy. Senator Fulbright noted,
"Universities might have formed an effective counter-
weight to the military industrial complex by strengthening their emphasis on traditional values of our democracy,
but many of our leading universities have instead joined
the monolith, adding greatly to its power and influence."[9] Yet it is often argued that the opportunity for
contact with the working frontier of national research
and development policy provides the only means through
which university scientists can be sufficiently knowledge-
able so as to influence such policy.

Universities are caught in the middle. The fact that
they do not have authority over off-campus laboratories
presents a "tricky weave of accountability issues."[10]
Critics of government-university arrangements contend
that university management of laboratories implies tacit
endorsement of activities over which they have no control.[11] They argue that classified research is not compati-
ble with academic freedom or with traditional patterns
of open communication in science, but others often inter-
pret these values to mean that a university should have a

[9] Senator J. William Fulbright, "The War and Its Effects,"
Congressional Record—Senate, December 13, 1967, p. S18485.
[10] Ruina, *op. cit.*, p. 125.
[11] Brooks, *op. cit.*, p. 955.

laissez-faire policy toward an individual's scientific activities and should allow a scientist to contract for any research he wishes. As a consequence of increasing controversy on these issues, several university administrations have been attempting to sever their ties with federal laboratories. M.I.T.'s decision concerning the Instrumentation Lab is a dramatic example.

The Instrumentation Laboratory

The Instrumentation Lab was conceived and developed by Charles Stark Draper, who remained its director until December 1969, when, in response to the controversy, his position was changed first to vice director and then to president of the laboratory. His philosophy and ideals dominate the character of the laboratory and delineate its activities (see Appendix I).

Draper, who was sixty-eight years old in 1970, is known to lab personnel as "Doc" and is often referred to as an "engineering genius" or "Mr. Gyro." His unique technical skills have played a major role in the development of guidance and control systems. The association of this charismatic, highly independent, and controversial figure with the Institute began when he was a student and has been maintained continuously. He became a full professor in the Department of Aeronautics and Astronautics in 1939 and an Institute professor in 1966.[12] His early work in the 1930's was devoted to developing instruments to measure vibration in aircraft engines and

[12] This position allowed him to stay on at the laboratory after the normal retirement age of sixty-five.

propellors. These early studies of applied problems convinced him that his career should be focused on "projects directed toward bringing complete subsystems into existence . . . including all essential phases ranging from imaginative conception, through theoretical analysis and engineering to documentation, manufacture, supervision of initial small lot production, and finally monitoring of applications to operational situations." [13] This conviction has guided the work and the organization of the Instrumentation Lab and its relationship to M.I.T.

During the 1930's, Draper recognized that military projects, with their well-defined objectives and adequate funding, were well suited to his systems approach. This fact, and his interest in aviation, led him to concentrate on control and guidance systems; his work in the 1930's was the basis of the inertial guidance systems developed fifteen years later.

Projects and Personnel [14]

Draper first received recognition for his development of a gyroscopic gunsight. Its success at the beginning of

[13] Charles S. Draper, "The Instrumentation Laboratory of the Massachusetts Institute of Technology, Remarks of the Director of the Laboratory from Its Beginnings until the Present Time," 1969, p. 9 (mimeograph).

[14] The following material is developed from interviews and from Charles Stark Draper Laboratory, *Annual Report* (Cambridge, Mass., January 1970). See also "Remarks by C. S. Draper" (Instrumentation Laboratory of the Massachusetts Institute of Technology, 1969, mimeograph).

World War II led to the establishment of The Confidential Instruments Development Laboratory, which received a contract to build gunsights for combat trials in the Pacific. Several models were developed, including the MARK 14, the number referring to Draper's ill luck from "standing pat" on 14 in the game of blackjack— a personal touch that has always characterized laboratory activities. Work on gunfire control systems shifted to airborne gunsights during the latter years of the war. When it became clear that the inability to control the motion of the plane was a limiting factor, flight control studies were initiated and continued to be a major concern of the laboratory.

Immediately following the war, the laboratory received its first contract to build, design, and test an inertial navigation system using gyroscopic instruments that could guide vehicles without reference to external points. Essentially, such systems involve the application of Newton's laws to determine precisely the velocity and position of a vehicle. The development of such instruments, called an "unforgiving art," requires high precision and predictability. The first system to employ inertial properties, called FEBE, was completed in 1948, followed by a fully inertial system, SPIRE, in 1953, and SPIRE Jr. in 1957. A self-contained navigational system for submarines was also developed in the early 1950's.

In 1956, Draper participated in discussions with the Department of the Navy on control and navigation systems for submarine-launched ballistic missiles. The laboratory had already been working with Convair to

develop an inertial guidance system for the Atlas Inter-
continental Ballistic Missile. That project, taken over
by the Air Force, was diverted to the development of
a system for an intermediate range ballistic missile called
THOR, and later to a project on guidance for the Titan
ICBM. On the basis of this work the Instrumentation
Lab received the Navy contract for the Polaris guidance
system. In line with Draper's systems approach, and supported by Navy contract policy, this was a "womb to
tomb" contract with complete systems and operational
involvement; the laboratory was to work out theory and
design, build engineering models, and test the system for
production. In the process, the I-Lab worked closely
with Lockheed, the prime contractor for Polaris, and by
July 1960 the first guidance system was complete.

Others followed: SABRE, a reentry system for long-
range ballistic missiles contracted by the Air Force in
late 1963, and the Multiple Independently Targeted Reentry Vehicle (MIRV) of the Poseidon missile. Because
of their controversial role in arms control, the three Poseidon contracts (two of which were completed by September 1970, and the third with an expiration date in
December 1973), were the main targets of the demonstrations against the I-Lab.

Other controversial projects were Army-supported
VTOL, a control system for vertical take-off and landing, and the Deep Submergence Rescue Vehicle, DSRV,
part of a high priority project of the Navy Oceanographic Program.

Still another series of projects began in 1961 with the

funding by NASA of the guidance and navigation system for the Apollo Command Module and the Lunar Excursion Module. By 1969, $108 million had been spent at M.I.T. on this project. Other NASA projects followed, and in 1969, NASA support of laboratory work totaled $28.4 million, or 52 per cent of the total contracts of the laboratory.

These are the major projects of the Instrumentation Lab. About 25 of the contracts, including parts of the NASA Apollo project that are significant for military application, have classified aspects. In 1968, 16 formal reports issuing from the I-Lab were classified and 70 were unclassified; of the engineering notes, 44 were classified and 88 were not. Thus, the distribution of 28 per cent of the total output was restricted to those with security clearance. Draper insists that military classification is less confining than the classification used to maintain proprietorship in competitive civilian development and that it does not hinder the transfer of basic information. But the requirement of "clearance" limits access to the laboratory; one needs a badge, an authorization, or a guide.

Major I-Lab programs and their sponsors are summarized in Table 5. In addition to the large-scale projects for the DOD and NASA, a number of smaller projects have been initiated at the laboratory in recent years and carried out in cooperation with various M.I.T. departments. A separate division of Scientific Technology was created in 1967 to manage the interdepartmental programs, which include collaborative projects in public transportation and air pollution.

Table 5. Major programs at the Instrumentation Laboratory, 1969 *

Project	Purpose	Sponsor
SEAL	Application of inertial locating equipment to survey and maintenance of airways navigation systems	FAA
Gyro Research	Continued development for increased performance and exploration of new methods	Air Force-ASD
Inertial Testing Technology	Investigation of inertial guidance testing and instrumentation methods	Air Force-MDC
SABRE	Development of self-aligning boost reentry system for advanced inertial guidance of long-range ballistic missiles and multiple independent targeted warheads	Air Force-SAMSO
DSS	Development of navigation for deep submergence vehicle	Navy-DSSP
Ocean telescope	Development of an array of thermistors and pressure transducers to measure spectral and synoptic characteristics of oceanic internal waves in main thermocline	Navy-ONR
Polaris	Design and fabrication of advanced inertial system	Navy-SSPO
Poseidon	Guidance for advance submarine launched vehicle	Navy-SSPO
Apollo	Overall responsibility for design and development of navigation and guidance systems	NASA-MSC
Advanced Command Guidance and Navigation System	Study and preliminary design of advanced techniques for guidance and control of manned deep space vehicles	NASA-MSC
Bearing Research	Development of material-optimized ball bearings for spin-axis application for space gyroscopes	NASA-MSC
SIRU	Development of a structure-mounted inertial reference unit assembly for use in the Apollo Applications Program	NASA-MSC
Inertial Component Development	Development of an advanced gyro and accelerometer	NASA-ERC
Orbiting Astronomical Observatory	Development of a system for precision attitude control of an orbiting astronomical observatory	NASA-GSFC
VTOL control	Development leading to velocity control system for vertical take-off and landing	Army-AVLABS

* M.I.T., Charles Stark Draper Laboratory, *Annual Report* (Cambridge, Mass., January 1970).

Draper's preference for long-term, large-scale projects, to be carried through from the initial development of theory to an operating system, precluded reliance on grants for basic research. Most contracts were large: in the fall of 1969, the twenty-nine largest projects brought in a total of over $52 million and employed 765 staff personnel. The largest of these, Apollo, was funded for $18,200,000 and had a professional staff of 225. Indeed, two of these twenty-nine projects had contracts of over $5 million each, four had funding ranging from $2 to $5 million, and five were between $1 and $2 million. In addition, twenty-six minor projects were funded for a total of $1 million. Sources of support in selected years are shown in Table 6.

Table 6. Sources of financial support of the Instrumentation Laboratory, 1959–1969 *

Agency	Fiscal 1969	Fiscal 1967	Fiscal 1965	Fiscal 1959
	%	%	%	%
Air Force	$ 7.2 (13.2)	$14.3 (29.6)	$13.9 (35.2)	$ 8.9 (62.3)
Army	0.5 (0.9)	0.8 (1.7)	0.5 (1.3)	
Navy	17.3 (31.7)	14.9 (30.8)	6.9 (17.4)	5.3 (37.0)
NASA	28.4 (52.0)	18.0 (37.2)	17.7 (44.6)	
AEC	0.3 (0.6)			
FAA	0.3 (0.6)	0.3 (0.6)	0.6 (1.5)	
Industrial	0.6 (1.1)	0.2 (0.4)	0.2 (0.5)	0.1 (0.7)
Total	$54.6	$48.4	$39.7	$14.3

* Information Sheet distributed to Pounds Panel (mimeograph).

Each of the Instrumentation Laboratory programs was carried on in a separate, autonomous project group in one of sixteen buildings, and this decentralization was responsible both for the strength of the I-Lab and for its lack of flexibility. Limited communication among the project groups inevitably resulted in duplication. But autonomy served as an incentive for high performance, for group leaders were entrepreneurs, responsible for their own more or less self-contained domains. The laboratory was able to maintain itself as a loose federation, first because of Draper, who presided over the entire operation, and, second, because of the M.I.T. umbrella. Both appeared as essential to the continuing viability of the I-Lab as a cohesive unit.

In 1969, the entire structure was managed by a staff of 75; 3 deputy directors, an executive officer, 3 directors for outside relationships (education, scientific collaboration, and advanced technology assessment), 22 associate directors in charge of project groups, and 41 deputy associate directors. Finally, there were 5 special consultants, 3 of them professors in the Department of Aeronautics, the department to which the laboratory was formally attached.

Of these 75 key personnel, 59 had worked with Draper for more than ten years, 43 of these for more than fifteen years, and 23 had been with the Instrumentation Lab for twenty or more years, virtually since its inception. In other words, the laboratory has had a large stable core of people whose entire career development had been closely associated with Draper's interests and the laboratory's special capabilities. This personnel history significantly affects flexibility, which is, in any case, limited by laboratory policy stating, "Projects must fulfill the condition that they lie in fields for which the laboratory has special capability because of past tasks successfully completed and the interests of ranking staff members." [15]

Out of a total of 2,448 employees in 1969, the laboratory employed 713 technical personnel trained as follows:

Electrical engineering	37.2%
Mechanical engineering	15 %
Aeronautical engineering	10 %
Physics	8.4%
Mathematics	9.5%
Miscellaneous	19.8%

Resident Navy, Air Force, and NASA engineers work at the laboratory along with technical representatives from the industrial manufacturers. In January 1970, there were 82 resident employees from industry and government. In addition there are numerous visiting technical personnel, for Draper believes strongly that the basis of engineering success lies in a close working relationship among all parts of a system. Since 1954, military sponsored visits by industry and government engineers have totaled 534,359 man days, averaging 2,783 man days per month; 465 companies have participated in these visits, including many that do subcontracting for the I-Lab. The balance between in-house and subcontracted work involving basic design is a delicate and sometimes controversial one in the laboratory, for contracting such work out tends to weaken in-house capability and may

[15] Charles Stark Draper Laboratory, *Annual Report*, 1970.

add to the cost of a project. This continuing relationship
between the laboratory and private industry led to the
establishment of thirty new technical companies between
1950 and 1965, a process that has been cited as having
a significant impact on the economy.[16]

How are projects brought to the I-Lab? Here it is
sometimes difficult to distinguish the role of the contracting organizations from that of the laboratory. Draper
and various group leaders generate the projects to be
researched, demonstrate their feasibility, and then seek a
contract to carry the idea through to the actual building
of engineering models. Draper has stated, for example,
that the laboratory's demonstration of the feasibility of
inertial navigation systems "provided an essential factor
in the Navy decision to start design and construction of
the Polaris system." [17] His membership on the Air Force
Scientific Advisory Board and his role of consultant with
the Army Scientific Advisory Committee placed him in
an optimal position for influencing the direction of military technological development.

[16] A study of these and spin-offs from other federal laboratories affiliated with universities is described by Edward B.
Roberts, "A Basic Study of Innovators; How to Keep and
Capitalize on Their Talents," *Research Management*, 11 (1968),
249–266.

[17] "Remarks by C. S. Draper," *op. cit.*, p. 23. The laboratory
project referred to is SINS, the Submarine Inertial Guidance
System. Other technical factors in the Navy decision were the
extrapolation of feasible yield-to-weight ratios for thermo-
nuclear warheads, the controllability of the combustion of
solid propellants and the feasibility of underwater launching
(Harvey Brooks, personal communication).

DSRV and MIRV

To illuminate some of the reasons for growing disatis-faction with the Instrumentation Laboratory, let us look briefly at two major projects, the Deep Submergence Rescue Vehicle (DSRV) and the laboratory's most controversial program, MIRV. The DSRV, a project of the Deep Submergence Systems group at the laboratory, is a high priority part of the Navy Oceanographic Program. Contracted as a rescue vehicle for use in disasters such as the sinking of the Thresher and the Scorpion, the DSRV is a 35-ton submersible vessel able to transfer up to twenty-four men and cargo from one submarine to another without their having to surface. There are two major prime contractors, the M.I.T. Instrumentation Lab and Lockheed Missiles and Space Company.

John Craven, former head of the Navy Deep Submergence Systems project, had helped to direct the DSRV contract to the laboratory in 1969. He was a visiting professor in the Departments of Ocean Engineering and Political Science at M.I.T. in 1969–1970 and was unofficially involved in guiding DSRV work. The original contract for a navigational system was followed by a series of contracts for design and control systems, for a computer, and for a program to integrate the system. The project group worked on every aspect of the DSRV including the training of the crew and participation in the sea trials.

There were few financial limitations in the early stages of the program and no need to justify expenses. From

1966 to 1969 the project grew from a group of five people with an idea to a 300-man program with an average $5 million yearly budget. In its peak budget year, 1968–1969, funding reached $10 million. With such rapid growth, inefficiencies were inevitable. A degree of waste and inefficiency is inherent in technological development, for there are limits to what can be anticipated and rationally planned.[18] The complexity of the DSRV mission, with its many sophisticated technical areas, posed a huge problem in technological management, and the project manager had constant difficulties with coordination. For example, the various systems were designed for the vessel by different groups, and insufficient space was left for cabling; integration of the systems became a major problem. Then, by the time the project was complete, there was little money left for adequate documentation, the expensive but essential process of drawing up reports and blueprints.

Critics of the DSRV program have claimed that the rescue vehicle is a cover for military research.[19] They

[18] A study by the U.S. General Accounting Office indicated that the estimated cost of the total DSRV program had increased from its original estimate of $100.2 million for six vehicles to $204.3 million for two. This was attributed largely to the fact that insufficient prior design work had led to unrealistic original estimates. U.S. General Accounting Office, *Deep Submergence Rescue Vehicle*, Staff Study, February 1971; and Comptroller General of the United States, *Report to Congress*, February 20, 1970.

[19] See *SACC Newsletter*, October 31, 1969, and Leonard S. Rodberg and Derek Shearer (eds.), *The Pentagon Watchers* (New York: Anchor Books, 1970). Submarine deterrent sys-

feel that the small likelihood of a submarine accident occurring close to a port and at a depth on the continental shelf that would permit rescue could not justify the large Navy expenditure on research and development. The intention of the research appeared to critics to lie in the potential for investigating installations on the ocean floor and for allowing a submarine fleet to be increasingly independent of the need to surface. If an underwater weapons fleet could remain invisible, that is, could be serviced without surfacing, it would be less vulnerable. The DSRV is thus associated by some critics with the simultaneous development of ULMS, a new submarine-based undersea launching missile system, and of a deep submergence search vehicle capable of diving to 20,000 feet and of seeking out objects the size of a basketball on the ocean floor.

Another I-Lab project that drew harsh criticism is the Multiple Independent Reentry Vehicle (MIRV), the most recent concept in the development of high accuracy ballistic missiles. MIRV carries multiple warheads capable of hitting several targets as far apart as 100 miles. A MIRV payload can carry several nuclear weapons; a typical system might carry three individual H-bombs of about 170 kilotons apiece. By using separate warheads, the total yield efficiency is reduced, but MIRV is potentially a great deal more destructive than other missile systems since each warhead can be individually guided

---

tems are generally not as controversial as MIRV. The issue here tended to be the appropriateness of such work in a university laboratory rather than military use.

to a selected target. In this way, a small number of missiles may destroy many fixed offensive facilities. MIRV was originally projected as a response to an anticipated USSR plan to build an ABM system around Moscow; its purpose, according to its project manager, is "to improve the probability of penetrating a ballistic missile defense system by saturating it with many targets." [20] With its deployment, it is estimated that the number of separately targetable strategic warheads in the United States will have increased from 3,854 to 10,264.[21]

Critics claim that the deployment of MIRV will stimulate further escalation of the arms race, and it has been called a "watershed issue" for the maintenance of a strategic balance of force.[22] Some argue that it can destabilize the present balance in the arms race, perhaps leading to a situation in which one side will have a "first-strike capability" that would seriously weaken the retaliatory capacity of the opponent.[23] Others argue that the level of technology is such that new weapons serve no strategic purpose, only creating greater international tension and

[20] Samuel Forter, Poseidon Program Manager, "Comment on Poseidon and the MIRV," M.I.T. Faculty Advisory Group Position Paper, November 1969 (mimeograph).

[21] G. W. Rathjens and G. B. Kistiakowsky, "The Limitation of Strategic Arms," *Scientific American*, 222, no. 1 (January 1970), 20.

[22] *Ibid.*, p. 29. More recently it is argued that the MIRV genie is out of the bottle and it is too late to do anything about it.

[23] Herbert Scoville, Jr., *Toward a Strategic Arms Limitation Agreement* (New York: Carnegie Endowment for International Peace, 1970).

thereby increasing the risk of war.[24] Another criticism is that the budget for strategic forces is so high that it has an inflationary effect on the domestic economy and limits the money available for more constructive purposes.[25]

The work at the I-Lab was critical in the development of MIRV, since it dealt specifically with the missile's accuracy. M.I.T.'s association with such a controversial program, through its management of the laboratory, provoked student critics to label the Institute "a direct outpost of the Pentagon."

Relationship to M.I.T.

Draper's predilection for academia has kept the laboratory officially a facility of the Department of Aeronautics and Astronautics despite its almost total dependence on federal funds. He saw his laboratory as "bridging the gap between academic studies and professional practice" and he regarded the relationship as crucial, both to the quality of his work and to the implementation of the three objectives of the laboratory as stated in the annual prospectus.

1. Advancement of education, particularly for the transition phases that lie between formal academic courses and professional practice, in an environment without barriers between these phases in the progress of personal development.

24 Rathjens and Kistiakowsky, *op. cit.*, p. 27.

25 Seymour Melman, *Pentagon Capitalism* (New York: Mc-Graw-Hill, 1970), pp. 97–99.

2. Contribution to knowledge and techniques of science, applied science and technology.

3. Creation of operational components, subsystems, and complete systems, producible by industry, and with performance characteristics that represent pioneering capabilities for the nation and our society.[26]

As a part of the Aeronautics Department, the Instrumentation Laboratory pays some faculty salaries, primarily for research time. This amounted to $42,000, for example, in 1967–1968; in the same year, graduate student support totaled $111,000, 81 per cent of which went to the parent department. The I-Lab, in this way, carries 20 per cent of the salary burden of this department and 1.5 per cent of the total salary burden of the university. The laboratory is also closely tied to the Aeronautics Department through educational activities. In 1968–1969, the laboratory participated in 25 of the 83 courses offered by this department and, through these courses, had contact with 615 registered students. Since World War II, 987 theses have been related in some way to I-Lab projects, 184 of them completed at the laboratory from January 1963 to December 1968. Twenty-seven of these were classified. In 1968–1969, the thesis work of 19 doctoral level students was being supervised by laboratory staff. The Instrumentation Laboratory, then, is a large, productive organization, revolving around the career of one individual, integrally tied to M.I.T. both financially and educationally, but operationally independent.

[26] *Annual Report, op. cit.*, January, 1970.

The size of the I-Lab, its entrepreneurial independence, the character and application of its projects, and
its close working relationship with the defense establishment had long caused some skepticism both at the Institute and even among some people in the Department of
Defense. In 1964, Eugene G. Fubini, who was then
deputy director of Defense, Research and Engineering
in the DOD, suggested to Draper that the laboratory
was operating as an industry, and that this was inappropriate at a university. He urged Draper to move in the
direction of more basic research, in particular, to extend
the work in navigation to studies of mapping from satel-
lites. Draper was reluctant to take up this suggestion,
and following this episode, DOD funding temporarily
dropped from 61.25 per cent of the total laboratory
commitments in 1964 to 49.7 per cent in 1965. The
laboratory shifted to increasing its dependence on NASA
sponsorship, although its volume of military research
picked up again in 1967.

Within M.I.T., the administration appointed a review
committee in 1968 to investigate all the Institute's outside
commitments,[27] and this committee concluded that the
size, the complexity, and the nature of research in both

[27] The committee was headed by Gordon S. Brown, former
dean of engineering. The committee listed about one hundred
external commitments of three types: general membership in
organizations such as the American Association of Universities
that tied M.I.T. to other educational institutions; commitments
generated by a professor or a department, which often involved
outside funding; and commitments that were initiated by an
outside company.

Special Laboratories warranted further special study. During this period, public debate over the consequences of MIRV deployment drew attention to the I-Lab. Administrative concern with the laboratory, however, remained latent. It was not until 1969 that the issue of the university's relationship to the laboratory and the nature of the I-Lab's research was brought to center stage.

III / First Strike: The Research Stoppage on March 4, 1969

On March 4, 1969, students and faculty organized a research stoppage at M.I.T. to express the concern of scientists with the "misuse of scientific and technical knowledge." It was directed to the issue of military research on campus and the need for increased attention to domestic problems. For many years, speeches and discussion at the Institute had emphasized similar concerns. Jerome B. Wiesner, then university provost and in 1971 its president, had been science adviser to President John F. Kennedy from 1960 to 1963, and at that time he had stressed the disproportionate level of military research and development and the relative neglect of civilian problems. Reevaluation of both scientific objectives was a major theme in the public speeches of both Wiesner [1] and M.I.T. President Howard Johnson. In 1966, in his first speech as president of M.I.T., Johnson emphasized

[1] Jerome Wiesner, "Rethinking Our Scientific Objectives," September 26, 1968 (brochure).

the importance of the end results of teaching and research. "I believe that the general range of problems attacked by M.I.T. in the future will shift more and more to those that understandably affect the way in which our society lives, that this Institute will increasingly exert its power towards problems of human significance." [2] "Humane technology" was the theme of his 1968 commencement speech: "There are innumerable social issues to which we must respond with greater commitment and effectiveness than before." [3]

This concern was reflected in efforts to encourage educational change. Yet Institute administration maintained a *laissez-faire* policy concerning the direction of research, relying on entrepreneurs within the faculty to generate projects in fields of interest to them. Thus, the concern with domestic problems was implemented primarily in several relatively small research projects, such as the Urban Systems Laboratory. Military and space research and development, conducted primarily at the Special Laboratories, continued to predominate, a reflection both of past habits and of the relative ease in finding support for military work.

The thrust of March 4 was by no means directed against research or technology; nor did it contradict the concerns expressed by the administration. On the contrary, it was the search for new priorities in the use of technological resources that prompted the research

[2] M.I.T., *Report of the President* (Cambridge, December 1969), p. 4.
[3] *Technology Review*, July/August 1968.

stoppage and engaged the broad participation of a generally cautious scientific community in the associated events.

The Strategy

The idea of the research stoppage originated with three physics graduate students, Joel Feigenbaum, Alan Chodos, and Ira Rubenzahl in the fall of 1968. Their attempts to recruit support met with success, particularly among biology students, and a Science Action Coordinating Committee (SACC) was formed to deal specifically with the issue of defense research and other military-related activities on campus.[4] SACC's purpose was to generate research, action, self-education, and greater social consciousness. Tactically, the organization was committed to avoiding violence, and its members participated primarily in nondisruptive activities seeking forums that would provide a means for disseminating their political position. This stance placed SACC in an awkward position during later events sponsored by other student groups, for at the same time many regarded it as a "radical" group, it found itself on the "right" fringe of student activity.

SACC has little formal structure; there is no official

[4] Later SACC's objectives were broadened to include problems such as the limited availability of socially constructive research jobs for scientists, the role of science as a resource for society, the absence of technological responsibility to community needs, and the lack of an active role for students in determining the style of their own education. *SACC Newsletter*, 2, no. 4 (April 1970).

chairman and its membership fluctuates depending on the situation. A coordinating committee of about twenty highly committed students met regularly during its most active period, the spring and summer following March 4, 1969. In addition, a number of small study groups were formed on an *ad hoc* basis, publishing a newsletter and gathering material for public debate.

In planning for March 4, SACC solicited the endorsement of faculty members, which they hoped would encourage participation of eminent scientists throughout the country. By December, forty-eight prestigious names were listed as faculty sponsors of March 4, with nine representing the social sciences and the humanities.[5] The nucleus of a faculty organization already existed, although it was oriented to discussion more than to action. In 1968, "Group Delta" had been established by liberal antiwar faculty to deal with crises growing out of "the atmosphere of frustration, confusion, and hostility pervading America." [6] This group was revived as the Union of Concerned Scientists (UCS) in December 1968.

By March 1969 the UCS grew to include an estimated 300 members in the Boston area, about 100 of them from M.I.T. Subsequently, the organization met as a group only during crises, but some small special interest committees formed for purposes of "exploring individual

[5] The distribution of the membership was as follows; 9 from social sciences and humanities, 5 from biology, 13 from physics, 4 from chemistry, 4 from math, and 13 from various engineering departments.

[6] Jonathan Allen (ed.), *March 4* (Cambridge: M.I.T. Press, 1970), p. xii.

problems, correcting the misapplication of science, reordering priorities, and studying new problems to which science can be applied." [7] These groups produced pamphlets on CBW, ABM, and MIRV.

The UCS avoided discussing M.I.T.'s research activities and turned its attention to the national scene; in March 1969 it proposed: [8]

1. To initiate a critical and continuing examination of governmental policies in areas where science and technology are of actual or potential significance.

2. To devise means for turning research applications away from the present emphasis on military technology towards the solution of pressing environmental and social problems.

3. To convey to our students the hope that they will devote themselves to bringing the benefits of science and technology to mankind, and to ask them to scrutinize the issues raised here before participating in construction of destructive weapons systems.

4. To express our determined opposition to ill-advised and hazardous projects such as the ABM system, the enlargement of our nuclear arsenal, and the development of chemical and biological weapons.

5. To explore the feasibility of organizing scientists and engineers so that their desire for a more humane and civilized world can be translated into effective political action.

Even though the UCS avoided local issues and its stated philosophy was similar to that expressed by Jerome

[7] *Thursday*, October 23, 1969.

[8] "Against the Misuse of Science—An Appeal by MIT Scientists," *Bulletin of the Atomic Scientists*, 25 (March 1969), p. 8.

Wiesner and Howard Johnson, the organization never had the support of the M.I.T. administration. At the same time, the caution of the UCS brought it into conflict with SACC during the planning for March 4. Compare the above UCS proposals with the more specific proposals of SACC in March 1969.[9]

That the co-operative programs with military related research projects be terminated.

That the co-operative program disassociate itself entirely from any institution that is involved extensively in war-related research.

That no credit shall be given for any classified thesis, classified courses or for classified research.

That a board be established at M.I.T. to help faculty, staff, and students locate research and employment in non-military areas.

That all war-related research at M.I.T. be replaced with socially constructive research. By M.I.T. we include the Special Laboratories, Instrumentation and Lincoln Laboratories. M.I.T. should continue to operate these laboratories since they "play a significant role in the academic and educational pursuits of the Institute." What we are asking for is not that M.I.T. disassociate itself from these laboratories, but, on the contrary, that M.I.T. assume responsibility for the research that is conducted there.

That the government together with the scientific community establish mechanisms for planning and funding in a coherent way non-military research and development. Criteria for awarding funds should be based on:

[9] These proposals circulated in a mimeographed handout, have been condensed, selecting only those relevant to the interests of this study.

a) social and humanitarian necessity.

b) scientific standards established within each discipline.

c) long-range planning before embarking on research and training students in a given field.

That in the preparation of the National budget for fiscal 1970, all research funds for university research be allocated by NSF, NIH, NASA, and the departments of HEW, HUD, and the Interior.

That the Department of Defense (DOD) justify each of its contracts on the basis of their direct relation to military necessity.[10]

Despite the differences between SACC and UCS, and despite faculty doubt about the propriety of a work stoppage,[11] the two groups continued to work together, with the understanding that faculty and students would maintain two separate organizations. The work stoppage would be launched on the evening of March 3, with a series of lectures and discussions throughout the following day. The two groups would independently take charge of their own sessions.

The UCS was not comfortable with the tactic of calling for a research stoppage, but it would have been difficult to find a more effective vehicle for activating the academic community: scientists were virtually forced to take a position. The symbolism of the "strike" was important, for in the context of a strike, nonparticipation is a significant decision. Moreover a strike is, in

[10] Note the similarities of this proposal to the Mansfield Amendment (see page 126).

[11] Allen, *op. cit.*, p. xviii.

effect, a declaration that there exists an alternative basis
for authority in an institution, and that it lies in the
ability to mobilize. Threatening existing structures, it is
a tactic which forces a response. Although they used
the strike technique, both SACC and the UCS delib-
erately avoided calling March 4 a "strike," anticipating
the divisive potential of the symbol. They preferred to
see the event as a work stoppage to express the scientific
community's concern. Yet, significantly, the word
"strike" instead of "work stoppage" was immediately
adopted both by the press and by participants as well
as by opponents of the strategy. There was clearly a
widespread fascination with the possibility of embarrass-
ing the government with a Lysistratan demonstration.

The anticipated objections arose; they hampered but
did not stop the event. Physics Professor Jerrold Zacha-
rias and a group of eighteen faculty objected to the stoppage "as an act of protest with an implied prejudgment
on the questions at issue" and as a misrepresentation of
the "spirit of research" in a free academic community.
This group felt that the constructive purposes of March
4 would be jeopardized by the tactic. Professor of Nutrition Nevin Scrimshaw, along with twenty-three members
of his department, felt that a strike was "improper and
irresponsible . . . a naive and hardly useful action."
They recommended a "research-in" for "constructive
discussion." [12] A group of engineers held a "work-in,"
pledging to work a compensatory sixteen-hour day on

[12] *New York Times,* February 23, 1969, and letters in *The
Tech,* February 14, 1969, and February 25, 1969.

March 4 to "uphold the principles of academic freedom." This was part of a nationwide "work-in" coordi-
nated by a group at Argonne National Laboratories.
Jerome Wiesner questioned the utility of the strike action, proposing instead that scientists organize to contribute to arms control.[13] The plans evoked no response
from the Instrumentation Laboratory.

The Events

The opposition only created publicity and fostered
curiosity; and the events went on as planned. They
began on the evening of March 3 and continued through
the evening of March 4. Twenty-six people, including
eight M.I.T. faculty, eight faculty from other universities, five students, and several industry and government
representatives spoke over the two days; panels on related subjects were held on March 8.[14] An estimated
1,400 observers attended the evening panels but few
came from the Special Laboratories.[15]

For the most part the speakers expanded on the positions outlined by the UCS and SACC. Only one,

[13] Allen, *op. cit.*, p. xiv.

[14] Further sessions were held on March 8 on the social consequences of new developments in biology and medicine, on
the use of computers in the social sciences, and on applications
of technology to urban problems. See Roger Salloch, "Cambridge: March 4, the Movement and MIT," *Bulletin of the
Atomic Scientists*, 25 (May 1969); Allen, *op. cit.*; and *Science*,
March 14, 1969.

[15] Rumors circulated within SACC that mailings to these
institutions had been diverted.

William McMillan, a RAND Corporation chemist and adviser to Generals William C. Westmoreland and Creighton W. Abrams, argued for the continuing development of military technology at universities. He claimed that the academic community was not sufficiently concerned with national defense and reminded the audience that practical realities differ from academic ideals. "The sheep of the west and the communist leopard are arraigned [sic] on opposite sides of the arena—and the leopard is not about to change its spots." [16]

The UCS panels emphasized such general issues as nonmilitary research opportunities, the relationship of the academic community to government, and problems of arms control, noting particularly that intellectuals have a responsibility to involve themselves in the consequences of scientific knowledge. Noam Chomsky, professor of linguistics and an articulate activist, spoke of the responsibility of man for the foreseeable consequences of his acts. Howard Zinn, a Boston University political scientist, argued that "the call to disinterested scholarship is one of the greatest deceptions of our time, because scholarship may be disinterested but no one else around us is disinterested. And when you have a disinterested academy operating in a very interested world, you have disaster." [17] Extending this point, UCS speakers declared that military research in universities is not politically neutral, that it involves the university as a partner in the "military, industrial, scientific complex." This

[16] W. G. McMillan, in Allen, *op. cit.*, p. 19.
[17] Howard Zinn, in Allen, *op. cit.*, p. 62.

theme was expanded in a dramatic speech by the Nobel laureate, biologist George Wald, who spoke on the corrupting effect of the military establishment. The most specific proposals were made by Ronald Probstein, an M.I.T. mechanical engineer, who described the experience of the Fluid Mechanics Laboratory as a model for the possibilities of conversion to nonmilitary research. Probstein and others in his laboratory had originally worked in the field of high-temperature plasma physics directed toward problems of missile reentry. Using similar fluid mechanics and chemical kinetic concepts, they converted their area of research to problems of air and water pollution, desalination, and biomedical fluid mechanics.

The SACC panel focused specifically on M.I.T. and its "important role in the establishment, . . . in the military part of the establishment," and presented specific proposals concerning research at the Institute. "We have heard a series of extremely eloquent talks on a number of subjects that are impinging on the very fiber of our lives. . . . We are here to talk about what we have tried to do . . . and what we would like to see all of you people out there join us to do." [18] SACC's objective was to convert the Special Labs to projects with nonmilitary application. Attempts would be made to "reach" scientists and technologists within the laboratories to make them aware of the implications of their work.

March 4 indeed heightened the awareness of the academic community to the implications of military re-

[18] Jonathan Kabat, in Allen, *op. cit.*, p. 125.

search, but it also created sensitivity to the fact that this research would cause increasing dissent within the universities. For SACC's call to action was based on an important assumption: "Staying at M.I.T. means changing M.I.T. And if you change M.I.T., you're going to change the nation." [19] This assumption that the university could serve as a pressure point for national policy was basic to the strong impact of March 4 at M.I.T. and of similar programs at thirty universities throughout the country. The events at M.I.T. following March 4 can be viewed as a test of this assumption. It proved untenable.

[19] *Ibid.*, p. 131.

IV / *Reconnaissance:*
The Pounds Panel

Campus incidents during April 1969 fixed the attention of the M.I.T. community on the issues raised by the March 4 activities. Walt Rostow, who had been a professor of economics at M.I.T. prior to becoming chairman of the Policy Planning Council of the Department of State in 1961 and White House special assistant in 1966, was invited to speak at the Institute on April 11, but disruptions forced him to leave the podium. Then on April 15, students picketed the Instrumentation Lab, and rallies were held to publicize SACC demands. The dean for student affairs described a sit-in outside the president's office as "almost disruptive but technically nonobstructive." [1] The students planned a march to the Instrumentation Lab, but Draper and René Miller, head of the Department of Aeronautics, met the students and invited a group of them for lunch; the march turned into an open air discussion.

[1] Kenneth R. Wadleigh, "Report by the Dean for Student Affairs," in M.I.T., *Report of the President* (Cambridge, 1969), p. 509.

On April 21, SACC met with President Howard Johnson to demand a moratorium on all Instrumentation Lab research on tactical and strategic weapons, but he rejected this appeal. Pressed by the continuing political turmoil, Johnson did appoint a panel, to be chaired by William Pounds, dean of the Sloan School of Management. It was to review M.I.T.'s relationship to the Special Laboratories, the process by which new programs were accepted by the laboratories, the implications of laboratory programs for on-campus research and education, the appropriateness of their sponsorship by M.I.T., and long-standing policies and procedures with respect to public service obligations. During the study the university would accept no new classified projects, but existing military projects were to continue. The Pounds Panel was given one month to make recommendations concerning the future of military research at M.I.T.; in essence its task during this month was to balance the "responsibility of scientists" with the exigencies of running a university.

At first Johnson appointed eighteen members to the panel; but in response to pressures from SACC for broader representation, Noam Chomsky, professor of linguistics, and Jerome Lerman, a graduate student and SACC activist, were added. Though Chomsky was giving a series of lectures at Oxford during this time, his presence on the panel was considered so important that he was flown back to M.I.T. each week to attend the meetings. Then, to balance the "radical" position, two more members from the Special Laboratories were included. The 22-member panel, consisting of 10 faculty, 4 students, 4 members of the Special Labs, 2 members of the M.I.T. Corporation, one alumnus and one professor from Yale, a former member of the M.I.T. faculty,[2] expressed a wide range of opinion. The administration hoped to prevent polarization and to forestall student disruptions by publicizing the panel proceedings and soliciting opinions and participation from the entire M.I.T.-Cambridge community.

Faculty members, including those who had not sus-

[2] Members of the review panel were: William F. Pounds (chairman), dean, Alfred P. Sloan School of Management; Robert L. Bishop, dean, School of Humanities and Social Science; Philip N. Bowditch, associate director, Instrumentation Laboratory; Noam A. Chomsky, professor of modern languages and linguistics; Gerald P. Dinneen, associate director Lincoln Laboratory; Peter Elias, professor of electrical engineering; Edwin R. Gilliland, professor of chemical engineering; Peter R. Gray, alumnus; David G. Hoag, director of Apollo Group, Instrumentation Laboratory; Jonathan P. Kabat, graduate student of biology; George N. Katsiaficas, student of management; Irwin L. Lebow, group leader, Lincoln Laboratory; Jerome B. Lerman, graduate student of electrical engineering; Elting E. Morison, professor of history and American studies, Yale University; Frank Press, head, Department of Earth and Planetary Sciences; Marvin A. Sirbu, Jr., graduate student of electrical engineering; Eugene Skolnikoff, professor of political science; Gregory Smith, member of the M.I.T. Corporation; Julius A. Stratton, member of the M.I.T. Corporation and president emeritus; Wallace E. Van der Velde, professor of aeronautics and astronautics; Victor F. Weisskopf, Institute Professor and head, Department of Physics; Richard J. Wurtman, associate professor of endocrinology and metabolism, Department of Nutrition.

pended classes on March 4, now voted to call off classes on two afternoons in early May to permit discussion on "the issues facing universities." These "Agenda Days," included a panel called "Dialogue or Dissent" featuring M.I.T.'s vice presidents and deans. President Johnson introduced the events: "M.I.T. cannot belong to any of us alone, students, faculty, administrators, Corporation, or alumni. It belongs to each of us and to history," [3] a remark suggesting that the administration as well as the radical students saw M.I.T.'s stand as crucial to the direction of the nation. As a part of the Agenda Days, the local educational television station ran a debate on M.I.T.'s role in military research called "The Contemporary University in Society as seen from M.I.T." A five-minute segment of an Agenda Days session was carried on NBC news, in which Chet Huntley noted that SMILE, the Science-Military-Industrial-Labor-Education complex, was due for a change. Finally, the Pounds Panel announced a two-week session of hearings and encouraged all those interested to express their opinions in writing or in person. The panel received written communications from 247 individuals and, of these, 97 were from Instrumentation Laboratory personnel. One petition was signed by 236 I-Lab employees.[4] There were 39 letters from Lincoln Laboratory, and the remainder were from students, faculty, and alumni.

[3] *The Tech*, May 8, 1969.
[4] Another was signed by six Instrumentation Lab personnel. There were also petitions from the Lincoln Laboratory, one signed by 4 people, the other by 12 people.

The range of opinion and intensity of concern expressed in these communications indicate the complexity of the task undertaken by the Pounds Panel. Letters touched on weapons development, national policy, student activism, education, the moral basis of war, communism, and Vietnam, as well as personal employment concerns. The situation was further complicated by an ambiguity inherent in the role of a review panel. In preliminary discussions the panel had to decide whether the hearings should be public or private.[5] Was the panel primarily to gather information so that its members could form an opinion? Those who supported this view argued for executive sessions, claiming that open participation would be inefficient. Was the panel to be a channel for public evaluation? Was it to have a public information role? If so, open meetings were essential. Chomsky, for example, felt that the purpose of the panel was to "bring the relevant information to people who are concerned without their having to make a life work of finding it out . . . it is precisely at this point that the role of a review committee seems to me to be extremely important." [6]

Eventually there were both public and private sessions. One hundred and four people met with the Pounds Panel in twenty formal meetings.[7] In addition, panel

[5] "Hearings of the Commission to Review the Special Laboratories," April 27, 1969 (available in M.I.T. libraries).

[6] Ibid., May 8, 1969.

[7] Of the 104 people who met with the panel, there were 8 members of the administration, 31 M.I.T. faculty, 24 staff mem-

members traveled to Washington to interview Senator William Fulbright, John Foster, director of Defense, Research and Engineering, and Thomas Paine at NASA. Others went to California to consult with Herbert York, chancellor of the University of California at San Diego, Wolfgang Panofsky, director of the Stanford Linear Accelerator, and Harold Brown, former secretary of the air force and president of the California Institute of Technology.

Opinions

Recommended courses of action ranged from maintenance of the status quo to immediate conversion of the Special Laboratories to civilian projects. At this point, only a few people saw divestment of the laboratories as a desirable solution.

Despite their objections to the nature of the work in the laboratories, activist students did not want to separate them from M.I.T. On the contrary, they agreed with Draper about the educational value of laboratories with an orientation to "real" problems. But they argued that weapons research made M.I.T. "a key member of the military-industrial-university ménage à trois," a role that undermined the university as a "community of individuals committed to free inquiry, to critical analysis, to experimentation and exploration of a wide range of

---

bers and employees of Lincoln Lab, 13 staff members and employees of the Instrumentation Lab, 16 students, and 12 people from outside M.I.T.

ideas and values." [8] SACC believed that if M.I.T. ceased research contributing to militarization, the example would have a significant impact on national policy. For they noted M.I.T.'s access to the government, to the press, to industry, and to other universities.

The basis for the SACC position was clearly stated in a letter to Lee DuBridge, President Nixon's adviser for Science and Technology. SACC urged DuBridge to call for closer university ties with civilian federal agencies. "Too often has the concept of national security served as a *carte blanche* for bankrupt and sometimes tragic policies. Now the urgency of neglected social and environmental problems must claim the fullest attention of our intellectual and economic capabilities." [9] Their position was further elaborated in a report to the Pounds Panel by Jonathan Kabat.[10] To implement a program for converting the laboratories to civilian research, Kabat suggested establishing an interdisciplinary Department of Conversion Science that would work with the Special Labs to establish long-range strategies and to test methods of conversion.

In the light of subsequent skepticism about the possibilities of conversion, it it important to note that SACC did not call for an immediate change: "Such a process

[8] M.I.T., Review Panel on Special Laboratories, "Final Report," October 1969, p. 8.

[9] Letter from SACC to Lee DuBridge, January 14, 1969.

[10] Jonathan P. Kabat (co-signed by Noam Chomsky and Jerome Lerman), "A Personal Addendum to the Panel Report," in M.I.T., Review Panel . . . , "Final Report," October 1969.

is obviously a long-term commitment, and cannot be accomplished overnight, however desirable. We therefore expect that the laboratory will continue for some time with much of the defense work in which they are currently engaged." [11] SACC did ask, however, for termination of several of the more controversial projects.

UCS presented a similar plea for conversion, emphasizing at once both the dangers of unquestioning acceptance of DOD priorities and the necessity for maintaining existing research groups. Several ongoing projects were suggested as potential conversion models: CARS, an interdisciplinary transportation project involving six M.I.T. departments, and an ambulatory health care program at Lincoln Lab.

Some employees of the Special Labs, particularly from Lincoln Laboratory, were receptive to the challenges posed by conversion and welcomed the change in research orientation.[12] One letter suggested that security clearance in the labs be noncompulsory. Several Instrumentation Lab personnel suggested changes in work organization to allow individuals to pursue civilian applications of instrumentation research, which had been limited under mission-oriented contracts. One writer recommended that a fixed percentage of all contract money be invested in new projects in appropriate civilian areas. A position paper from six employees proposed the gradual introduction of a "contract quota system," in which

[11] *Ibid.*, p. 82.
[12] The unidentified quotes that follow are from letters received by the Pounds Panel.

research priorities would be established to regulate the amount of money fed into various categories. Some people justified military research by arguing that it fostered the development of techniques that could be applied to air and urban transportation, areas otherwise neglected due to public reluctance to allocate funds to domestic problems.[13] This argument of military research spillover was labeled fallacious by Kabat, however, who claimed that "the shroud of classification . . . can legitimately be taken as *prima facie* evidence that the justification of social utility is unreal." [14]

There were many who objected to any changes at all in the research orientation of the laboratories. Draper himself referred to the Pounds Panel investigation as an "inquisition," and many people in the Instrumentation Lab and in the Department of Aeronautics felt threatened by the procedure. A particularly bitter expression of this sentiment appeared in a position paper by Charles Broxmeyer, a deputy assistant director of the I-Lab responsible for the navigational system of the Deep Submergence Rescue Vehicle. "The committee should recognize that its existence, and the words spoken under its auspices, are a deadly threat to me and my colleagues." Broxmeyer dramatically compared the student unrest at M.I.T. to "McCarthyite hysteria." "The work of the

[13] R. H. Miller, "The Draper Laboratory and the Department of Aeronautics and Astronautics," February 24, 1970 (mimeograph).

[14] M.I.T., Review Panel on Special Laboratories, "First Report," May 31, 1969, p. D20.

committee and M.I.T.'s role will be judged in the same context as that of other tribunals. . . . The M.I.T. community, symbol of the rational conduct of human affairs, symbol of the power of science and technology, is indulging itself in the ancient rite of purification known as scapegoating." [15] Thus, he saw the laboratory and its employees as victims used to cleanse the guilt and fear of the students and faculty.

Laboratory employees, including draftsmen and technicians as well as academics and administrators, felt victimized and said so in letters to the Pounds Panel. Most were brief expressions of uncritical loyalty, both to their employer and to national priorities. "Leave if you don't like it." "The strongest offense is the only defense." "Only a militant minority objects to the lab." "Communist sympathizers." "Research is the last and only defense against communism overseas and in America today." "The Special Labs are necessary for the defense of freedom." Many letters were highly personal and dramatic: ". . . a knife in the back to me." "On behalf of my job . . ." The laboratory had employed and trained many immigrants who related personal stories of the opportunities that had been provided by the I-Lab and were angry and distressed by the threat to their security.

Two local unions buttressed this written response to the deliberations of the Pounds Panel; they were concerned about the impact of impending changes on their

[15] Charles Broxmeyer, "A Position Paper on the Committee for Investigating the Special Laboratories," n.d. (mimeograph).

membership. On May 4, 1969, the Building Service Employees International Union, Local 254, filed suit against M.I.T. The local had 6,500 members, 850 of whom worked at M.I.T. The suit, and a complaint filed with the National Labor Relations Board charging unfair labor practices, sought to bar M.I.T. from entering discussions that would phase out the laboratories, and proposed that the union participate in any assessment of the relationship of the laboratories to M.I.T.[16] "Thousands of jobs are at stake, not only at M.I.T. but in dozens of allied industries in the area." A clear distinction was made between the interests of the employees and the ideals of the students, "a group of pseudo-intellectual vagabonds." The Research, Development Technicians, Employees Union, an independent union of about 1,400 M.I.T. employees, also demanded assurance that any decisions would not affect their membership, and representatives went directly to Department of Defense officials in Washington to voice their concerns.

Some of the letters noted the importance of the I-Lab as a source of financial and educational benefit for M.I.T. and criticized students as naive. "The view that the students are suffering from an excess of virtue, whereas their elders are intellectually dishonest is a lot of rubbish. Students have no perspective. . . . They expect overnight transformation which in the nature of the case, can't take place if one understands history and the

---

[16] Statement by Edward T. Sullivan in the Boston *Globe*, May 4, 1969; Boston *Herald*, May 1, 1969; and *The Tech*, May 6, 1969.

element of human psychology." The Pounds Panel was opposed as an annoying and futile exercise. "If every new assault on the so-called establishment is to be answered with a panel with no long-range guides, then we face endless turmoil and confusion."

Specific projects were defended. For example, a petition from 236 Instrumentation Lab employees supported Poseidon.

We, the undersigned employees of the M.I.T. Instrumentation Laboratory, wish to make known our support for the continuation of design work on the Poseidon Guidance System. We believe that the Poseidon missile system is a vital link in our national defense and is the most effective nuclear deterrent weapon in the free world arsenal. We know that only by further improvement in this system, whether or not it is released for production, will guarantee that balance of nuclear power will remain in America's favor until such time that diplomatic channels can provide for total nuclear disarmament.

We further believe that it is logical and highly desirable that the Instrumentation Laboratory be involved in the Poseidon program because of the Lab's demonstrated technical competence, its ability to provide unbiased advice to the Navy, its minimal cost on the over-burdened economy, and its freedom from profit motivation. . . .[17]

Many employees responded predictably to student efforts to "reach" them. They referred to students as a small vocal group of "anarchistic trouble makers," and

[17] Petition from employees of the Instrumentation Laboratory (mimeograph).

"the eminent 'Mein Kampf' masters of the Machiavellian art, who, through long Castro-type harangues have managed to capture a handful of malcontents hell bent on the destruction of this great institution of higher learning." Would M.I.T. become "another notch on the gun of student militance?"

Letters from alumni tended to favor the existing relationship. One placed an interesting perspective on the function of a university by suggesting that M.I.T.'s overriding commitments are to national interests, because students are only present for several years while ties to the nation are perpetual.

Those interviewed from NASA and the Pentagon were skeptical of conversion possibilities.[18] "The human life span is about the time that society is willing to accept change," said Thomas Paine of NASA when questioned about the possibility of conversion. Harold Brown, former secretary of the air force, said he knew of no case where a laboratory devoted to one purpose had been successfully converted. He suggested that even if the Instrumentation Lab were better than an industrial equivalent, it was not completely unique; in other words, the government could get its work done elsewhere. And Robert A. Frosch, assistant secretary of the navy for research and development, noted the value to universities of work in advanced engineering technology.

Few people concluded that divestment would be the appropriate alternative. Those who sought to end M.I.T.'s military research commitment did not want to divest the laboratories, since permitting them to function

[18] "Hearings," May 9–10, 1969.

as independent corporate institutions would perpetuate exactly the kind of research they felt to be immoral. The only members of the Pounds Panel to explicitly recommend that the Institute divest the Special Laboratories were Marvin A. Sirbu, Jr., a graduate student in electrical engineering and Edwin R. Gilliland, professor of chemical engineering. They felt that the size and the established interests of the laboratories would make it difficult to shift the focus of research, and they suggested phasing out the laboratories and initiating new efforts in smaller, flexible groups. The laboratories, they felt, had developed an expertise based on their present style of operation. "To keep an administrative shell and a name, while changing almost everything else . . . would have the effect of destroying the laboratories as facilities capable of performing the missions for which they are now suited." [19] Thus, the possibility of divestment began to emerge during the Pounds Panel discussions but was not seriously considered at this time.

Consensus or Dissent

A former employee of the Instrumentation Lab summarized the moral, ethical, and military arguments presented both in support of and against the laboratory as "a fantastic cover up for the good old American way of doing business, namely porkbarrelism." The official report, however, sought a "golden mean." The members of the panel lived together in a suburban estate [20] for an

[19] M.I.T., Review Panel . . . , "Final Report," p. 46.
[20] Endicott House, Newton, Mass., owned by M.I.T. for conferences.

intense week during which they considered the opinions. The report and its recommendations were approved, often painfully, line by line. On May 31, 1969 it was submitted to President Johnson.

Recommendations were based on the assumption that the laboratories would remain a part of M.I.T. They were as follows:

1) The laboratories and M.I.T. should energetically explore new projects to provide a more balanced research program. . . .

2) The educational interaction between the special laboratories and the campus should be expanded. . . .

3) There should be intensive efforts to reduce classification and clearance barriers in the Special Laboratories. . . .

4) A standing committee on the Special Laboratories should be established . . . as a means of providing the President with the considered advice of students, faculty and laboratory staff.

Though emphasizing that military sponsorship presented a serious problem of imbalance that has hampered the ability to cope with social problems, the panel did not seek the ultimate elimination of all defense work. It concluded, however, that the Poseidon program "at this state in its development" was inappropriate for M.I.T. sponsorship and advised a review of future commitments to the program, while recognizing the necessity of honoring existing contracts. Until the proposed standing committee became operational, the panel recommended discontinuing the moratorium on new classified projects. They also set down very general guide-

lines for the acceptance of new programs: that they be
examined for their intellectual challenge, for their objectives and implications, for their costs and benefits to
all aspects of M.I.T.'s educational programs and resources, and their humane objectives. The attitudes of
the M.I.T. community were also to be taken into account.

The May version of the Pounds Panel report, signed
by all members of the panel, suggest that the participants generally agreed with these conclusions, although
appended statements by Chomsky, Kabat and Lerman
indicate their reservations. For this group, the vagueness
of the recommended guidelines belied the stated intention to convert. They viewed the decision about Poseidon as academic, since Draper had made it clear that the
Poseidon project was essentially completed and that remaining contracts were primarily for trouble-shooting.
They also predicted that the generality and moderacy of
the panel recommendations would result in ineffective
action, a position reflecting the generally cynical view
of commissions held by many activists. This view, col-
ored by familiarity with the long-neglected findings of
national commissions, assumes that even when commissions are advisory in nature they are in fact used to
mobilize support for policies already determined.[21]

Other panel members thought that although M.I.T.

[21] There is a literature which supports this point. See for
example, Don Price, *Government and Science* (New York: Oxford University Press, 1962) and Harold Seidman, *Politics, Position and Power* (New York: Oxford University Press, 1970).

should have divested the Special Laboratories many years earlier, it was now politically unwise to take such action. Some participants believed eventual divestment inevitable, though probably not for four or five years. Thus, in large part, consensus on the report's conclusions was based on pragmatic consideration of political feasibility.

Later, in the final report, appearing in October 1969, Chomsky, Kabat, and Lerman retracted their earlier support, stating categorically their basic disagreement with the panel conclusions. George Katsiaficas, a student in the School of Management who was originally placed on the panel as a moderate, added his voice to the dissent. "I do not object to these proposals for change as much as to the spirit in which they were promulgated and received: the Panel's initial report served as a justification of the status quo. To many of those concerned with the cancerous growth of the Special Laboratories . . . radical change in the nature of the projects of the Special Laboratories is necessary for the laboratories to remain an integral part of the university." [22] Katsiaficas had been "radicalized" over the summer and was increasingly involved in activities designed to force radical change.

Draper's response to the recommendations, which were made public on May 31, was immediate: he announced to the Boston *Globe* that he would "consider other alternatives" if his laboratory's effectiveness as a unit was threatened,[23] and that a policy change would

[22] M.I.T., Review Panel . . . , "Final Report," p. 90.
[23] Boston *Globe*, June 6, 1969.

force him to cut ties with M.I.T. and "seek support through other channels." The *Record American* ran a headline "Lab Chief will fight MIT Report." [24] Draper was unwilling to break apart laboratory groups whose future success was predicated on past experience and expertise in the substantive area of guidance control.[25] He noted the many possible applications of work in instrumentation technology, describing how the I-Lab had contributed its expertise to M.I.T. departments when precise instrumentation was required. He cited, for example, the development of the GDM Viscometer, an instrument for measuring tiny torques, or twisting forces with a high level of precision, which permitted fine measurement of the viscosity and flow properties of blood. Draper claimed that civilian projects require ideas generated from within a research group. Such a group requires exploratory money to begin to develop these ideas before it can raise significant funds, and there is, he insisted, simply no source of government funding for such exploratory projects. Further, the problems in civilian technology are "economic and political" rather than technological, and the concern of the laboratory,

[24] *Record American,* June 6, 1969.

[25] There is some literature that indicates that interdisciplinary research teams can in fact be converted effectively. I. M. Levitt of Stanford Research Institute describes a program in which a team brought together to work on an aerospace program was transferred to produce a device useful in medical education. I. M. Levitt *et al., Some Major Impacts of the National Space Program,* 7 (Menlo Park: Stanford Research Institute, September 1968), 27.

he noted, was the development, not the use, of technology.

The response of the press was mixed. *Air Force and Space Digest*, a magazine of the aerospace industry, viewed the report as "a clear-cut acceptance of the arguments of Chomsky and his allies" [26] and noted elsewhere that "if the universities turn their backs on the real world of international conflict, unpleasant as that world is, they will lose a major portion of the relevance they are so consciously seeking these days." [27] In contrast, the *New York Times* viewed the report as "a significant contribution to sanity and social responsibility. . . . The Report is admirable as evidence that confrontation tactics have not yet entirely elbowed rationality out of formation of university policy." [28] The editorial commented that allowing a more effective voice for students and faculty can be beneficial, "when all elements proceed with a genuine desire to arrive at consensus instead of polarization."

While there was no immediate administrative action, Jack Ruina, the vice president of the Special Laboratories, noted in his *Annual Report* that the university had obligations to those employed in the laboratories, that change would affect the financial organization of the university, and that defining war-related research

[26] William Leavitt, "The Dethronement of Dr. Draper," *Air Force and Space Digest*, December 1969, p. 48.

[27] William Leavitt, "Revolt on the Campus: Against War Research," *Air Force and Space Digest*, 52 (June 1969), 76.

[28] *New York Times*, June 4, 1969.

and an appropriate role for a university were difficult problems. Ruina emphasized that time was needed to confront these problems, and he questioned whether the Institute could evolve a "rationale for all seasons" that would clarify its public service role.[29] Thus, the first administrative response was pessimistic about the possibility of significant change.

[29] M.I.T., *Report of the President* (Cambridge, 1969–1970), p. 678.

V / Accommodations and Negotiations

The Pounds Panel report left the administration caught between the pressures for reform and the economic and political imperatives of running the Institute. The idea of divestment was beginning to emerge, but before the administration came to that decision, it made some awkward efforts to explore alternatives.

The M.I.T. Academic Council, a group of senior academic and administrative officers with a major decision-making and advisory role at M.I.T.,[1] met early in September 1969 to discuss the Pounds Panel report. They concluded that the spring events and the report called for a dramatic response, and as a result, on September 18, the Executive Committee of the M.I.T. Corporation endorsed an intensive program for implementing the recommendations of the Pounds Panel. These recommenda-

[1] The Academic Council includes all Institute deans, faculty officers, and vice presidents. It meets weekly as an entire group and is responsible for the budget, all responsibilities delegated to it by the President, and all business brought to it by its membership.

tions "should have the President's high priority and should have a major claim on his time in the next few months." The committee agreed "that it would be inappropriate for the Institute to incur new obligations in the design and development of systems that are intended for operational deployment as military weapons." This was qualified, however: "This is not to mean that, with its unique qualities, the Institute should not continue to be involved in advancing the state of technology in areas which have defense applications." [2]

President Johnson attempted to clarify the Executive Committee statement.

The laboratories will continue to do fundamental research and to develop new technology in the field of communications optics, guidance and control . . . [and] will continue to do exploratory work on new systems concepts including those with important defense applications. However, the Laboratory will not assume responsibility for developing operational weapons systems based on these concepts, nor . . . for the field testing or production of special weapons systems.[3]

Johnson's reasoning, outlined in his statement to the faculty on October 22 (Appendix II), emphasized that there were potential problems in implementing the

[2] M.I.T., *Report of the President* (Cambridge, 1969–1970), p. 3. The text of the Executive Committee Statement is in President Howard W. Johnson's "Statement on the Special Laboratories, October 22, 1969" (see Appendix II).

[3] Howard W. Johnson, "Statement on the Special Laboratories, October 22, 1969," M.I.T., *Institute Report*, October 24, 1969. The complete text of this statement is in Appendix II.

Pounds Panel recommendations, although some of these problems were still not clear. He asked for faculty support to test their feasibility during the 1969–1970 academic year, noting that he believed his plans to be in the best interests of government sponsors, of the Special Laboratories, and of M.I.T. He received an overwhelmingly affirmative vote of 650 to 11.

Johnson warned that funding for large-scale technological involvement in domestic problems would be difficult to secure; the government was already cutting federal research expenditures. He indicated that if changes in the direction of research were likely to reduce the effectiveness of the laboratories, the possibility of separation could not be excluded.

Guidance and Guidelines: The Sheehan Committee

In September, the standing committee recommended by the Pounds Panel was appointed to evaluate the acceptability of specific contract proposals from the Special Laboratories, to gauge the likelihood of early implementation of the panel's recommendations, and to act as a communications link between the laboratory, the administration, and the M.I.T. community.[4] The committee was headed by John C. Sheehan, Dreyfus Professor of Organic Chemistry, and included, as recommended by the Pounds Panel, 4 faculty, 2 students, 2 administrators, and a staff member from each laboratory.[5]

[4] "Interim Report of the Operations of the Standing Committee on the Special Laboratories," May 12, 1970 (mimeograph).

[5] Members of the committee were Peter Elias, professor of

In its primary task of reviewing contract proposals, the committee faced the vagueness of the guidelines proposed by the Pounds Panel. What criteria could be used to evaluate the acceptability of a scientific research project? SACC members insisted that research projects be consonant with the goals of an institution of higher learning, and in the best interest of society. Similarly, the UCS asserted that the effect of a project on the university, the extent to which research is openly available, and its consequences for the community and the nation must all be considered.

But how could these guidelines be implemented? Was it valid to reject proposals on the basis of their stage in operational development? The Pounds Panel had concluded that further work on Poseidon was inappropriate on this basis. Kabat, on the other hand, labeled that decision a diversion, claiming that the only valid issue was one of military intent.[6] But evaluating a project according to whether it is intended as an offensive or deterrent weapon raises further problems of defining which weap-

---

electrical engineering; Andrew Gilchrist, III, third-year student, Department of Chemistry; Robert L. Halfman, deputy head, Department of Aeronautics and Astronautics; David G. Hoag, associate director, Instrumentation Laboratory; Michael J. Marcus, graduate student, Department of Electrical Engineering; Edward W. Merrill, professor of chemical engineering; Walter E. Morrow, Jr., assistant director, Lincoln Laboratory; Carl F. J. Overhage, professor of engineering; and Hans-Lukas Teuber, head, Department of Psychology.

[6] M.I.T., Review Panel on Special Laboratories, "First Report," May 31, 1969, p. D21.

ons are in fact offensive and which are deterrent. This in turn involves predicting the potential use of a weapon in varying political and military contexts.

These questions were complicated by the ambiguity of the concept of academic freedom. What are the implications of attempting to establish criteria beyond the substantive validity of a research project? And what are the limits of an individual's freedom to bear sole responsibility for his work? On the one hand, an engineering professor argued that researchers are in fact free to follow their own interest. "I have been free to pursue my interests and fortunately they have coincided with the interests of a granting agency. If they did not, of course, I am still free to pursue these interests, with my own money." [7] Others denied that this situation ensured the free and "disinterested" pursuit of knowledge and also argued that the exchange of ideas necessary to academic freedom was inhibited by security clearance.[8]

The Sheehan Committee developed procedures whereby ambiguous guidelines could be applied to specific proposals. Before a laboratory submitted a proposal, its representatives presented project summaries to the committee along with oral briefings. Each committee member evaluated the suitability of a project by rating it with respect to nine factors: the potential for favorable interaction with M.I.T.'s educational operations; the unique-

[7] Sheldon Penman, "The Relation of Quasi-Educational Structures to the University," 1969, p. 9 (mimeograph Position Paper).

[8] M.I.T., Review Panel on Special Laboratories, "Final Report," October 1969, p. 34.

ness of the M.I.T. contributions; the degree to which projects would evoke favorable M.I.T. attitudes; the intellectual challenge; the national importance of the problem; the degree of basic research represented as opposed to production, field test, and deployment; the absence of immediate identification with a weapons system; the adequacy of existing national review of the problem; and the potential for civil application. In addition, each member wrote a substantive statement. About 100 Instrumentation Lab proposals were reviewed by the committee in this fashion, one-quarter of which were extensions of ongoing projects. There was disagreement within the committee on about 15 of the proposals. The committee did not attempt to reach unanimity on individual projects, but the difficult cases were delayed by the review process and some were still pending when the decision to divest the I-Lab was announced. One problem was that classified portions of the cases were inaccessible to the review committee, and some members felt that "projects whose nature and objectives, at least, could not be disclosed should not be proposed or accepted." [9] The committee as a whole recommended that the Special Laboratories make every attempt to reduce classification barriers.

The committee itself, however, operated in closed session and its reviews were privileged material, a procedure justified as necessary for obtaining the confidence of laboratory personnel. It was feared that indiscreet disclosure of the review material might trigger a move to-

[9] "Interim Report," *op. cit.*

ward divestment at a stage where this had been neither explored nor recommended.[10] In fact, the committee's relationship with the Instrumentation Laboratory was strained; those whose work was controversial were sensitive about the potential reaction of their sponsors. Carl Overhage, one-time director of Lincoln Lab, claimed it "unlikely that laboratories . . . will be long supported by the government if their activities in fundamental research are not combined with the development of systems that are suitable for operational employment." [11] Instrumentation Lab personnel called the committee the "peoples' court" and the "morals committee," and many felt that the review procedure was intolerable in view of the laboratory's need to maintain coherence and continuity for project employees.

On the other hand, SACC criticized the unequal representation of students on the committee, the fact that faculty members were appointed rather than elected, and especially the closed proceedings. SACC referred to the committee as "elitist," "secretive," "illegitimate," and as an example of the "authoritarian and undemocratic nature of MIT." A new Poseidon contract had been submitted in June 1969, after the Pounds Panel had labeled the project inappropriate but before the Sheehan Committee review procedure was established. SACC re-

[10] Interestingly, the report in which this concern was expressed was sent to the president on May 14, only one week before the administrative announcement of the divestment decision and well after the decision had been made.

[11] Carl Overhage (a member of the Sheehan Committee), Position Paper, 1969.

garded this as an act of bad faith on the part of the administration, an interpretation strengthened by the refusal of the administration to release the dates of defense contracts.[12]

On March 3, 1970, 150 students confronted the committee at its weekly meeting, claiming that "closed doors" were contrary to the Pounds Panel objectives and demanding greater participation in the review process. Again, on March 9, a group of students tried to organize a "people's lobby" to protest the Sheehan Committee's secrecy, but this aroused little interest and the meeting deteriorated into a popcorn party. Meanwhile, the committee resisted the continuing pressure to release information.

Redeployment: Changes in the I-Lab

In late September, President Howard Johnson announced that the name of the Instrumentation Laboratory would be changed to The Charles Stark Draper Laboratory and that on January 1, 1970, Dr. Charles L. Miller, head of the Department of Civil Engineering and director of the Urban Systems Laboratory (USL), would replace Draper as director. Draper would remain as vice director, responsible for guidance and navigational programs. The change would "acquaint those agencies charged with solving problems of growing national concern in transportation, urban development, pollution and the like with the laboratory's capabilities,

[12] *The Tech*, October 14, 1969.

and thus achieve the more balanced program urged by the Pounds Panel." [13]

Miller, as director of the USL, represented a program relevant to social issues, though one which operates at the comparatively small scale of about $1 million annually. By appointing him, the administration gained time without yet making firm commitments. The Urban Systems Laboratory was already co-sponsor of several projects with the Instrumentation Lab. It could be absorbed into the laboratory and at the same time provide a funding base from which to develop new projects. Miller would continue to seek funds from such agencies as the Department of Transportation (DOT), and Health, Education and Welfare (HEW), just as he had been doing all along as director of the USL. The only change, from his point of view, would be an increased emphasis on air traffic control, a natural activity for the Apollo group. This possibility of conversion was cut off, however, when the DOT decided to centralize its Cambridge research funding and to divert most of its research budget to a new central facility located at the site formerly planned for NASA.

Miller maintained his old office in the USL and never moved to the Instrumentation Laboratory. In an interview with a journalist from the *Air Force and Space Digest*, he stated his intention to maintain military commitments while building up the civil sector to the level of military and space research over a period of five years.

[13] M.I.T., *Report of the President* (Cambridge, 1969–1970), p. 41.

He estimated that from $10 to $15 million per year would be needed to develop such a civilian research program.[14]

Also in January, Jack Ruina, vice president for Special Laboratories, resigned and the position was abolished. The responsibilities were delegated to a newly created position of vice president for research, and Albert G. Hill, professor of physics, was appointed to administer research at M.I.T. Like Ruina, Hill had long experience with military research, having been director of the DOD weapons systems evaluation group, a consultant to the Army, Navy and Air Force, and a member of the President's Science Advisory Committee (PSAC). He also had been at Lincoln Laboratory in the early 1950's.

The decision to replace Draper was announced early in September in an attempt to take action before the students returned to make further demands concerning the work in the laboratory. But the reaction to the change was miscalculated; not only those who supported Draper but also the activists received the news with bitterness and skepticism. A reporter from *Air Force and Space Digest* called the "dethronement of Dr. Draper" a "triumph of reverse McCarthyism" and a response to a "coterie of self-appointed zealots." "For all practical purposes they have won. Only the mopping up operation remains." [15] Draper, who had not planned to

[14] "Laboratory Issue Polarizes Faculty," *Aviation Week and Space Technology*, December 15, 1969, p. 55.
[15] William Leavitt, "The Dethronement of Dr. Draper," *Air Force and Space Digest*, December 1969, p. 48.

retire until June 1970, was bitter and stated publicly that he did not resign but was fired. He asked the Corporation to rescind its limitation on new contracts for weapons systems, claiming the laboratory could not live with such a restriction. Draper focused his resentment on the administration; when introduced by Johnson at an M.I.T. Corporation dinner, he refused to acknowledge the gesture. While he would help in the search for sponsorship for civilian projects, Draper declared his profound misgivings about the possibilities. "You've got to have vision, if you're going to have a viable thing you just don't take in small jobs like washing—you've got to keep your eye on the mountain peak, as we've done in the past. You've got to have the ideas first, not pay a lot of people to come up with them." [16]

Within the laboratory, morale was a major problem. An across-the-board pay raise of 10 per cent helped, but the administrative changes were a slap in the face. Signs were posted around the buildings: "Doc Draper forever, SDS Never!" A Boston employment firm, Technical Horizons, Inc., began interviewing laboratory employees in October for possible placement in other positions.

Interestingly, student activists also opposed the replacement of Draper and doubted that it would involve any major policy changes. SACC viewed the move as an internal reorganization intended to pacify students and as a token substitute for real analysis of conversion pos-

[16] "Dissent Focuses on Instrument Lab," *Aviation Week and Space Technology*, December 1, 1969, p. 72.

sibilities. They felt that it was not Draper, but M.I.T.'s policy that remained an obstacle.

In November, SDS students produced what they felt was evidence to support their doubts, a "liberated" memorandum dated October 21, 1969, from Charles Miller to President Howard Johnson.[17] They distributed the memorandum as a leaflet headlined "Conversion, their Version, Dear HoJo." In the memo, Miller noted that present difficulties in funding the Urban Systems Laboratory were going to involve phasing out support for faculty and student participants in USL projects. While this was happening "it appears that a one million dollar Ford Grant to convert the Special Laboratories will be announced and enforced." This combination of circumstances, Miller claimed, would be met with hostility and interpreted as a reaction to radical activity and as an example of "the wrong ordering of priorities by the administration."

> Putting Ford money into a lab where no one seems to see a crisis situation, when dedicated faculty and students are being cut off in USL, is something I cannot understand and will not be able to defend. I personally feel that the Special Lab grant is a mistake and one which is going to backfire on the administration. . . . I have become painfully aware of the very serious pressure and morale problems associated with the Instrumentation Lab. While wide use

[17] November Action Coalition, "MIT Lab Conversion: The Ford Fraud Exposed," n.d. (mimeograph). The Ford proposal was submitted but was not awarded.

of Ford funds can help ease some of these, I feel it would be a mistake to ignore the critical needs of USL while giving a misleading illusion of "converting" the Instrumentation Lab.

Torn between two responsibilities, Miller was concerned about the competition for limited funds. He advised the president to exercise care in announcing the Special Laboratory grant and to schedule the proposal so that the Urban Systems Lab would be assured of renewal support from Ford. Miller publicly acknowledged his authorship of the memo and justified it in terms of his primary concern that the Urban Systems Laboratory with its 50 faculty and 150 graduate students maintain its autonomy and its educational priorities.

At this time there were several indications of administrative ambivalence. Despite Draper's feelings, he and President Johnson issued a joint statement,[18] declaring that the laboratory "continues to conduct defense-related research, and, at the same time to devote its competence in high technology to urban and other domestic problems. There is basic agreement between us as to the policies of the Laboratory." Several other documents appeared in *Thursday*, a student newspaper. In a letter to concerned alumni in early January, Johnson wrote:

There is no sense here of "converting" the laboratories to urban problems. There are some major problems in air traffic control, transportation and health services that are consistent with the Laboratories' mission . . . we would not weaken its fundamental purpose . . . we have not

[18] *The Tech*, October 24, 1969.

yielded to minority pressures on these matters, much less radical minority pressures.[19]

The students interpreted these documents as confirmation that the conversion policy was illusory, that support for conversion research was unlikely, and that there was no shift in M.I.T.'s overall research priorities. "It is clear that M.I.T.'s conversion policy is merely a facade to ease the very serious pressure of popular opposition while furthering the profitable enterprise of defense-related research." [20] Miller claimed that by the time he actually assumed the directorship of the laboratory in January 1970 he was aware that a decision had already been made to divest the Instrumentation Lab.[21] This decision, however, was not to be publicly announced until the following May.

This entire phase of the political process marked a change in administrative strategy. The administration had hoped that an open decision-making process might diffuse dissent. There was an enormous profusion of rhetoric representing all possible points of view, far more than could be incorporated into any decision. By September, the administration assumed that implementing the Pounds Panel recommendations required a high degree of expertise and a minimum of public controversy. "The committee's business simply cannot proceed in a climate

[19] *Thursday*, January 16, 1970.

[20] November Action Coalition, *op. cit.* Also, an editorial in *The Tech* on November 12 speculated that there was no intention to convert and that the I-Lab would in fact be divested.

[21] Personal interview.

of perpetual referendum and even less in the setting of mass meetings with their attending clash of potentially irreconcilable opinions." [22] "It is not possible for a university to be run like a New England town meeting," said David Truman with respect to Columbia.[23] In any case, activists, even when invited to participate, by now assumed that their participation would have no impact; they saw other routes as more effective in influencing the university.

[22] "Interim Report," *op. cit.*, p. 10.

[23] Jerry L. Avorn, *Up against the Ivy Wall* (New York: Atheneum, 1969), p. 59.

VI / Student Offensive:
Confrontation and Crisis

During the period when student disruptions were a regular occurrence on many campuses, there was little political activism among students at M.I.T. except for a few incidents related to recruitment and the draft. A dramatic change in the political atmosphere on campus took place in the fall of 1968, when the Cambridge branch of a national draft resistance organization, Resist, used an M.I.T. building as a sanctuary to protect an AWOL serviceman. In the spring of 1969, the voice of the left was articulated in a new publication *Up against the Wall Street Journal*, open to anyone who wanted to express "biased opinion." There followed a "publishing implosion" as political expression became a popular student activity. Two new weekly papers, *Thursday*, an "independent community newspaper," and *Ergo*, representing conservative opinion, appeared.

Student activism was not confined to national political issues. Undergraduates criticized the traditional student government (Ins Comm) as irrelevant and nonrepresentative, and in 1968–1969, several student groups of-

fered proposals for a new student government. Those
who had supported the Resist sanctuary proposed a
participatory system, one which would provide leadership for the students concerned with social and political
action. On March 13, 1969, Ins Comm was dissolved
when undergraduates voted a new student government
constitution for a "unified university." This established
a General Assembly of seventy-five students with pro-
portional representation from various residential groups.
Michael Albert, who had emerged as an activist in the
events of 1968, campaigned for the presidency, promising to enlist the support of students to end war-related
research if he won. He was elected by a close vote, 655–
617, after a controversial campaign in which he was first
disqualified because his student status was ambiguous,
and then reinstated.

Student organizations proliferated and a number of
minor events began to polarize the community. These
led to a second phase in which events escalated to the
level of a crisis. With the involvement of various student
organizations, the range of concern broadened well beyond the particular activities of the Instrumentation Lab.
Military research at M.I.T., however, remained the central political issue in the student protest.

Organizations

In the spring of 1969, toward the end of the Pounds
Panel deliberations, SACC began to reconsider its strategy. Frustrated by the "procedural haggling" and the
"elliptical language" of the Pounds Panel report, the

students resolved to focus on specific demands that would lead to "constructive reconversion of our society." [1] They proposed leafleting, picketing, and public demonstrations as tactics for gaining student support. On June 16, at the Annual Alumni Homecoming, SACC called a rally that culminated in a public argument between students and alumni. This was the only spring demonstration, however, for the plan was to formulate a political philosophy and "to hammer out our political differences." The students decided to distribute responsibility and decision making broadly within SACC and to mobilize a network of students throughout the M.I.T. community to allow quick response to new developments.

During the spring of 1969, another student group entered the arena, the M.I.T. branch of the Students for a Democratic Society. MIT-SDS had formed in the winter of 1968–1969 to attack two disparate issues: the working conditions of maintenance men at M.I.T. and the misuse of science and technology. In June, they distributed leaflets denouncing the Pounds Panel report as "a slimy load of administrative propaganda" and noted that it was published in a nonunion shop by "scabs." Other leaflets claimed that the Pounds Panel never came to grips with M.I.T.'s role as a "servant of U.S. imperialism" and predicted that conversion would mean "domestic counter insurgency and social control research."

By late spring, some student radicals were still trying to work with the faculty. In a series of letters Michael

[1] *SACC Special Newsletter,* May 26, 1969.

Albert referred to the faculty as "middlemen," asking, "Don't you share my anger and frustration? Don't you desire to work hard and long, not on 'business as usual,' but at rebuilding this sick society? . . . Let your objective neutrality be damned. . . . Neutralism is partisan." [2] But the UCS, which had sponsored March 4, was to become almost invisible during the political action of the fall of 1969.

Albert also wrote a proposal to the Ford Foundation asking for $17,500 to study the place of the university in society. He claimed to have received some encouragement from the foundation, contingent on M.I.T. sponsorship, but the Academic Council refused to back the project. Activity ceased during the summer as students dispersed, but as soon as classes resumed in the fall, campus opinion began to polarize.

The split in SDS at the national level occurred during the summer of 1969, and it was reflected at M.I.T. in two factions of the organization, MIT-SDS, and Rosa Luxemburg SDS (RL-SDS). Though both groups were opposed to military research on campus, they differed in their strategies for changing existing relationships. The MIT-SDS position was based on its goal of "a worker student alliance to end oppression of the working class." [3] To attack the I-Lab was, they claimed, "phony militance." The laboratory was an inappropriate and short-sighted target; employees would be threatened by obstructive tactics designed to convert the research. MIT-SDS concluded that the target of the student movement should be the administration, "which controls the research and profits from it," and that demands should focus on abolishing specific war-related projects and protecting laboratory employees.[4] Thus, while this faction continued to oppose administrative policy on military research, it dissociated itself from many of the student activities of the fall of 1969.

As an action-oriented organization that viewed the issue of military research as a way to mobilize the left, RL-SDS was far more involved. The group had no clearly defined membership; participation in meetings and events varied with the context, and coherence was provided largely by committed activists including Michael Albert. Though his interests as the General Assembly president had previously included curriculum reform, ROTC, and other issues, he now chose to focus singlemindedly on war-related research.

Another RL-SDS activist was George Katsiaficas, the student in the Sloan School of Management who had sat on the Pounds Panel. Although he had once been a conservative student and member of the Interfraternity Council, his contact with Jon Kabat and a series of "intellectual and emotional experiences" during the summer of 1969 had changed his perspective.[5] In the spring

[4] MIT-SDS, "To Fight War Research-Fight Administration, Not Workers," 1969 (mimeographed handout).

[5] *Thursday*, October 9, 1969. Katsiaficas had worked for the Birdseye Division of General Foods, where he became disaf-

he had objected to the disruption of Walt Rostow's speech; several months later he was threatening disruption of the entire university. By the fall of 1969, his name was modified by the phrase "newly radicalized."

Prompted by the activities of SACC and the SDS, conservative campus groups flourished. The Young Americans for Freedom (YAF), a national group that had been organized in support of Barry Goldwater's presidential campaign, announced a 40 per cent rise in regional membership for the fall of 1969.[6] The most articulate backlash came from a group called the Society of Radicals for Capitalism.[7] Its philosophy, heavily axiomatic, austere, and authoritarian in tone, reflected the influence of Ayn Rand. Its spokesman, James Meginnis, advocated the principle that reordering national priorities was a question to be left to free market demands:

It seems long overdue for someone to point out to the establishment that the government . . . should confine its activities . . . to the efficient application of retaliatory force through its armed forces, police forces and legal system. If this concept of government were generally understood, the question of "reordering our national priorities" would no longer be an issue. . . . The free market would

---

fected by the "inhuman climbing and scratching for promotion."

[6] M.I.T. branch of YAF had sponsored a "tactical weapons contest" to encourage the invention of nonnuclear weapons in the spring of 1968 (*Technology Review*, May 1968).

[7] The Society of Radicals for Capitalism distributes 5,100 free copies of *Ergo Newspaper* weekly to the M.I.T. community.

embrace all the positive activities of men. The concept of national priorities as understood in the conventional sense presupposes a government which exceeds its proper bounds and actively intervenes in the market.[8]

Radicals for Capitalism viewed those who opposed war-related research with scorn. In a cartoon entitled "New Paths for MIT," radical-left students are quoted as saying "the capitalist imperialist government pigs are dictating our lives to support their power lust to control the workers and students of the world!! We demand that SACC control the corporation, that SACC control the people, that SACC . . . War is peace, freedom is slavery . . . Down with I Lab . . . Down with MIT Branch Post Office . . . George Washington was a Fascist pig!!" In articles, heavily underlined for emphasis, the Institute was criticized for allowing the radical students to win by default. "Weather: cancelled by order of SACC, meteorologists will receive normal pay." "The confident look on the demonstrators' faces came into sharp focus. The answer was *there*—there in the Pounds Panel report, in the success of the militants in affecting the policy of the I Lab." [9]

In October an emeritus professor organized a "Stop the Paint" club, after the facades of several buildings and hallways were painted with antiwar slogans. To prevent any further "invasion," he recommended an "informal vigilante watch committee." [10] One student responded: "Bigger crimes than the desecration of build-

<hr>

[8] *Ergo,* October 15, 1969   [9] *Ibid.*
[10] *Thursday,* October 2, 1969.

ings are occurring every day in Vietnam and I would be guilty of disoriented values by letting the former crime concern me more than the latter." [11] A technological solution helped to resolve the problem as scores of bulletin boards appeared to cover the bare gray walls in M.I.T.'s endless corridors.

Happenings [12]

Alignments crystallized around a series of events that were to affect the administration's management of the Instrumentation Lab decision. Several minor episodes occurred in the early fall of 1969. On September 7 RL-SDS disrupted an alumni officers' conference. Michael Albert and seven other students snake-danced around banquet tables chanting "Ho Ho Ho Chi Minh" and then engaged alumni in debate. Later, the faculty committee on discipline found the group guilty of disrupting free communication. The committee placed five of the students under "admonishment" and Albert on disciplinary probation.

On September 15, Albert, as president of the undergraduate Assembly, spoke to the incoming freshman class, attacking M.I.T.'s support of "imperialism" through campus war research. At an organizational meeting of RL-SDS a week later he warned that the cost of continuing war research at the "second Pentagon"—i.e.,

[11] *Ibid.*

[12] Unless otherwise indicated the following events have been reconstructed from reports in the *Technology Review, The Tech,* and *Thursday* for 1969, and from interviews.

M.I.T.—would be higher than the cost of ending it, and plans were made for a city-wide action in November. This admonition was repeated in a statement to the Boston *Globe* on October 5.

Meanwhile SACC, using similar rhetoric but dissimilar tactics, published factual material on M.I.T.'s financial interests, corporate investments, and the multiple involvements of specific faculty members in the "military industrial complex." [13] It held a teach-in on September 25, but the administration did not participate and attendance was small, never exceeding 200. SACC's verbal position was threatening. In urging class cancellation on Moratorium day, October 15, the students announced that if M.I.T. did not cooperate, they would "be forced to conclude that M.I.T. is part of the enemy which must be destroyed if humanity is to survive on this planet." However, the organization continued to be cautious about the escalating pace of radical student activity.

On October 3, the M.I.T. Corporation held its annual meeting, and consideration of the Pounds Panel report was on the agenda. One hundred and fifty students marched from the Massachusetts Avenue entrance of M.I.T. a quarter of a mile away. At first only one student, a member of SACC, was allowed to address the Corporation. Then three students, including Albert, were allowed in, and finally twenty students entered the meeting room while the rest of the group listened to the proceedings through a public address system. In spite of

[13] "MIT and Military Capitalism," *SACC Newsletter*, September 26, 1969.

"noise, confusion and profanity," the corporation carried on its business and accepted the Pounds Panel report. However, the episode and the threats of disrupted classes alienated moderate students who felt that their rights were violated by "politically motivated crimes on campus" and who threatened to sue for tuition refunds if classes were affected.[14]

On October 10, about 150 students from RL-SDS marched to the Center for International Studies (CIS) in a peaceful protest against war-related research. There is no classified research at the CIS, but three projects were attacked as contributing to "psychological warfare": COMCOM, a program to develop computer simulations of international communication patterns especially in the Soviet Union and China; International Communism, a project to document the development and interaction of Communist parties and revolutionary movements; and the Cambridge Project to apply computer facilities to social science research. Dramatizing their power to occupy and obstruct, students announced that this was a "test" occupation. They were particularly irritated by Ithiel D. Pool, professor of political science and director of COMCOM, for his outspoken position on the Vietnam War,[15] and several weeks later, Pool, Max Millikan, professor of economics and director of the CIS, and William E. Griffith and Lucien W. Pye, both professors of political science and senior staff members of the CIS,

[14] *The Tech*, October 7, 1969.
[15] November Action Coalition, "MIT and Imperialism," November 1969, p. 8 (mimeograph).

were tried by a mock revolutionary tribunal and found guilty of "crimes against humanity." [16]

By this time, issues and tactics were becoming hopelessly confused, and this confusion was compounded by the formation of the November Action Coalition (NAC) of antiwar groups, the organizational expression of Albert's threat of city-wide action. As plans for the November Action crystallized, the movement fragmented.

The most vocal opposition to the November Action came from MIT-SDS as they continued to focus on the threat to employees inherent in any direct attack on the laboratories. "The Instrumentation Lab workers—and most of them get screwed by MIT—see this as an attack on them. . . . The I-Labs are not where the decisions are made." SACC also voiced concern. "Demands for cessation of projects must always be coupled with demands for worker security and retraining. A movement strong enough to stop projects should be strong enough to guarantee workers' jobs." [17]

That laboratory workers did not differentiate among student groups was obvious at a six-hour meeting sponsored by the laboratory to discuss the impending November Action. Seventy per cent of the audience was from the I-Lab, and speakers ranged from Draper to a member of the Weathermen. Draper was received with a standing ovation, in sharp contrast to the hissing and taunting

[16] *Technology Review*, December 1969, p. 96G.
[17] Ira Rubenzahl and Marco Saraceno, "Strategy Paper for SACC," fall 1969 (mimeograph).

epithets that greeted speakers from student organizations. I-Lab representatives elaborated on the theme that men, not technology, were at fault. William Denhard, associate director of the I-Lab, decried the "attempts to lay guilt at our doorstep for the world's problems" and he noted philosophically (quoting Konrad Lorenz) the animallike violence and selfishness basic to the character of man. He was followed by the president of the Technicians' Union, who spoke for his constituency.

Students presented their diverse perspectives. While MIT-SDS talked of a worker-student alliance, Marian Deldado [18] of the Weathermen warned, "The I-Labs are not going to be safe again." An RL-SDS speaker outlined the proposed November strategy of nonviolent picketing and closing offices.

Crisis and Control

The three-day November Action marked the high point of tension in the relationship between the administration and student activists. The administration expected the worst, but the menacing character of the November Action lay largely in its rhetoric. SACC, which refused to endorse the NAC because of their disagreement over tactics, had referred to the Institute as "part of the enemy that should be eliminated." Michael Albert, speaking for the NAC, called for demonstrations "to put an end to the machinations of the second Penta-

[18] She was accompanied by three other Weathermen. Draper later claimed that the Weatherman was "Bernadine Dohrn accompanied by three strong men."

gon." Another spokesman for NAC called for "militant disciplinary action" against M.I.T. Yet, RL-SDS, the main organizer of the NAC, claimed that there was no intention to do physical property damage or to initiate violence, and the NAC specifically rejected Weathermen proposals for violent action. Within these limitations, however, the intention was to obstruct military research activity.

As November approached, the Action gathered support from a bizarre mélange of Boston area organizations, including the New University Conference, a national organization of faculty, graduate students, and staff; the Weathermen; the Panthers; Bread and Roses, a women's liberation organization; a Peace Corps group; SDS chapters from other schools in the area; and the Executive Committee of the Interfraternity Conference. MIT-SDS refused to participate; SACC did not join the action but used the occasion to carry on parallel activities to disseminate its point of view.

Meanwhile, at a faculty meeting on October 22, Johnson said that "any acts by individuals or groups that coerce other individuals or groups from speaking or acting freely are considered to be fascist tactics. We would be acting irresponsibly if we did not prepare ourselves in the face of such explicit statements." He asked for and received faculty support that would allow him great leeway for administrative action in case of violence.[19] The administrative strategy at this point was influenced by the events of April 9–10 at Harvard during

[19] *Institute Report,* October 24, 1969.

which President Nathan Pusey, without faculty support, had called in the police in response to seizure of the administration building by about three hundred students. Over four hundred police had charged the building, and the results in terms of injuries and divisions within the faculty and among the students were disastrous. The Harvard experience and the hope to avoid the mistakes of the Pusey administration was a key factor in shaping M.I.T. administrative actions.

On October 28, the General Assembly voted 34 to 20 to condemn any action to forcibly eject M.I.T. personnel from their place of work and to support calling in civil authorities in case of violence. Rumors circulated that I-Lab employees were carrying bats, chains, and pistols. Guards at the I-Lab were in fact armed, but many of them were old, retired policemen, and one source of concern was that they might suffer heart attacks in any confrontation with students. The NAC claim that they would not initiate violence [20] was simply not believed. On November 2, the university announced a temporary restraining order issued by the Middlesex County Superior Court, enjoining the use of force or violence, damaging or defacing facilities, converting without authorization any files, or converging within any buildings so as to disrupt normal functions. NAC asked that this order be dropped, arguing that it was based only on rumors of violence and that it threatened freedom of speech; the request was refused.

[20] This denial was specifically made in their leaflets and to the press.

Emergency organizations appeared. An information center run by undergraduates was open twenty-four hours a day, and President Johnson, now referred to by students as "HoJo," reportedly was among those who called the center for information about what was happening on campus. The attempts to maintain communications also included public briefing sessions by Provost Jerome Wiesner and others, while Johnson himself avoided direct personal confrontation.

Another student group formed to accumulate information on legal processes, and the NAC took its own emergency precautions, advising its members how to react to the "pigs."

At the time of arrest . . . memorize your arresting pig's badge number. Don't talk with pigs! Answer questions about yourself—name, address, age, occupation, etc. Answer no questions about the Action, what you're charged with, or the Movement. . . . Decisions about how to defend ourselves in court legally and politically will have to be reached collectively. Ultimately, the only defense is the success of our Movement.[21]

Communications were also facilitated within the faculty by an *ad hoc* group of faculty advisers, one from each department. This group met regularly with some students who had been appointed by the dean for student affairs. A special Faculty Council meeting was called and an extra edition of *The Tech*, the undergraduate student newspapers, carried a report that the "faculty

[21] *Technology Review*, December 1969, p. 96G.

and administrative attitude has hardened . . . and there is widespread sentiment that police should be stationed on campus." [22]

On November 3, a special meeting of the faculty supported the temporary restraining order by a vote of 344 to 43, despite the misgivings of some faculty members who felt that it also threatened those who agreed with the goals though not with the tactics of the NAC. That evening about 300 students, including NAC representatives, participated in a "light a candle for peace" vigil and presented a petition signed by 1,700 people opposing disruption and violent confrontation. Yet, the next morning, November 4, a headline in *The Tech* read "Institute Hurtles Toward Violent Confrontation."

The planned action began at noon on November 4 with a rally at the Student Center. A group moved to the Hermann building, housing the Center for International Studies, where a mock revolutionary tribunal found members of the Center guilty of crimes against humanity. Estimates of the number of participants varied from a campus patrol figure of less than 250 to the *New York Times* figure of 1,000.[23] SACC had called a separate meeting at 10:00 A.M. and sent several representatives to talk to Provost Wiesner. Other SACC members joined the central activities, attempting to dissuade NAC from taking violent action. Both the NAC and SACC marched to the Instrumentation Lab, and then the group dispersed.

During the evening of November 4, the NAC was ad-

[22] *Ibid.*   [23] *New York Times*, November 6, 1969.

vised as to city rules regarding pickets, including the stipulation that picketers must keep moving and remain at least three feet apart. At 6:55 the next morning about 350 demonstrators [24] left the M.I.T. Student Center, where they had spent the night, and marched to Building 5 of the Instrumentation Lab, which housed Poseidon research. Laboratory employees had been instructed to carry on "business as usual" and most of the employees went to other buildings, but at 8:00 A.M. the city solicitor of Cambridge and a member of the Young Americans for Freedom who was not an I-Lab employee were knocked down when they tried to enter Building 5. A final effort to avoid confrontation with the police was made by Jerome Lettvin, professor of biology and a UCS activist, who pleaded with the students to disperse. The students ignored him, and newspapers carried a photograph of Lettvin in tears as two hundred Boston and Cambridge police, their badges removed, marched in at 9:10 A.M. The laboratory was reopened at 9:45 A.M.

Most news reports indicated that the police showed considerable restraint and noted the differences between this episode and the more violent experience at Harvard the previous April in which 41 students and 7 police were injured, and 197 students were arrested. Howard Johnson appeared personally at a Cambridge police roll call to thank the men for their behavior. However, 10 students, according to the M.I.T. Public Relations Office, were treated for injuries and one was arrested. The

[24] Only 20 to 30 per cent were from M.I.T., according to Provost Office estimates.

NAC announced its success in stopping, if only for a brief period, work on a war research project.

The next day, November 6, began with a joint SACC-NAC rally in Kresge Auditorium and a sit-in outside the president's office which was dispersed by campus police without incident. During the day, activists engaged as many people as possible in discussions in corridors, in local Cambridge stores, and in classrooms. The November Action ended with a faculty meeting at which several NAC members attempted to speak. Salvidor E. Luria, professor of microbiology, asked that the faculty modify rules on nonfaculty speakers for the occasion, but the faculty refused by a narrow margin to permit a dialogue at this time. A separate informal meeting of about one hundred professors was held because "we felt it was time for the faculty to pick up the ball—not just accede to the President." [25] This group attempted to bring the discussion back to the issues by proposing a strong public statement by the faculty against the deployment of MIRV. Physicist Philip Morrison brought this proposal before the faculty later in the spring, and President Johnson appointed a commission to consider the proposal. Chaired by Robert Solow, professor of economics, the commission met only once, in January 1971.

Following the November Action, President Johnson appointed two special panels. The first was to review complaints concerning acts during the demonstration that might have violated accepted standards of behavior and to submit recommendations regarding the rights and

[25] *New York Times*, November 6, 1969.

responsibilities of members of the community.[26] A second was to advise the president on the legal aspects of the November Action.[27] The first panel noted that only a small part of the M.I.T. community had been involved in the Action, either actively or passively; normal activities were pursued by most of the community. The events did, however, threaten the "trust and goodwill which tied together much of our University community" and were costly at a "time of change, experiment, examination of priorities and modification of resources." Unable to agree on a definition of obstructive behavior, the panel did not recommend that participants in the I-Lab picketing be given disciplinary review. Nor did they recommend disciplinary review of leadership, organization, or verbal threats of violence. They claimed that the diffuseness of such activities and the complex dynamics of leadership precluded such review, except in the case of individual actions.

The second panel found several of the events obstructive, but not destructive. Demonstrators, the panel concluded, showed restraint in response to the court order and no legal action should be taken. But ultimately five individuals were charged with individual actions: one was admonished, two were placed on probation, and Michael Albert, who was already on "admonishment," was expelled.

The anticipation of violence had been worse than the

[26] This group consisted of 6 faculty, 2 staff, 2 graduate students, and 2 undergraduates.
[27] This panel included 3 faculty, 1 staff, 1 graduate student, and 1 undergraduate.

fact, but interpretation of its significance and its effect on the normal operation of the Institute varied. Did it involve merely a handful of dissenters? Or was there in fact wide participation by M.I.T. students? Were individual events effectively obstructive? Was it an action of "idealistic and constructive reformers frustrated by what they hold to be the failure of effective democracy" or was it "concerned with rebellion for its own sake and with a consequent destruction of social and political institutions"? [28]

The varying interpretations reflected the confusion of issues and tactics. The question of research priorities at M.I.T. interested many students, including those with moderate inclinations. Indeed, a poll of the student body in December suggested considerable awareness of the issues.[29] Of 2,100 students who voted, 70 per cent opposed MIRV, 50 per cent felt that M.I.T. should get out of its weapons research commitment in any way possible, 44 per cent favored conversion, 14.5 per cent favored the present relationship, and only 3.6 per cent wanted to divest the laboratories. But NAC tactics themselves diverted public attention away from the substantive issues.

[28] "Report of the Panel of the November Events and the MIT Community," December 5, 1969, pp. 13–14. One rumor was that events had been instigated by outside agitators from Cornell. Alan Chodos and Joel Feigenbaum, two of the student organizers of March 4, had come from Cornell with Professor Kurt Gottfried, who was visiting professor in the M.I.T. Physics Department for a year.

[29] *The Tech*, December 18, 1969.

Issues Revisited

In early December 1969, SACC made an elaborate attempt to refocus attention on military research by joining with the Fund for New Priorities in America [30] to sponsor a national conference at M.I.T. on social and economic conversion. SACC tried to involve local industries that had military contracts and to use the conference to generate practical conversion proposals. A special issue of the *SACC Newsletter* introducing the program defined conversion as the "transfer of technological and economic resources from war-related projects to ones of social merit" and emphasized that the separation of the laboratory from M.I.T. would preclude meaningful change.[31] SACC was aware of the obstacles, however, and concluded that "a truly effective conversion requires changing the structure of our economic and political institutions."

The conversion conference attracted well-known speakers from universities, labor unions, industry, community groups, and from Congress. Indeed, the program looked like the table of contents for the *New York Review of Books*.[32] However, the conference was anticlimatic, attracting few who were not already com-

[30] The Fund for New Priorities is a New York City–based organization of liberal businessmen, who have funded several antiwar programs primarily of an educational nature.

[31] *SACC Newsletter*, December 3, 1969.

[32] Speakers included John McDermott, Paul Goodman, Nathan Hare, Ernest Mandel, Harvey Swados, and Seymour Melman. See *SACC Newsletter*, December 3, 1969.

mitted to SACC and failing to generate workable ideas
that could serve as the basis of a program. Following
the conference, SACC became comparatively inactive:
"Events since the conversion conference have been dis-
heartening." [33]

Christmas vacation brought a respite, and it was during the holiday that the faculty committee on discipline
recommended the expulsion of Michael Albert. The announcement, made when the students returned, stimu-
lated scattered vandalism—an iron pipe was thrown
through a window of President Johnson's campus home.
Albert's political activities were rumored to be the reason for his expulsion, and the student newspaper called
the move "a dangerous precedent, a threat to the rights
of students." Albert's father defended his son's actions
and Albert, himself, responded: "For those at M.I.T.
who dislike my politics because it threatens their interest, . . . all I can say is tough shit." [34] On January
13, 1970, the Undergraduate Assembly called the expulsion "political repression" and demanded Albert's rein-
statement. And the next day an "ultimatum" was presented to the provost demanding that past disciplinary
action be rescinded and that the disciplinary committee
be abolished. The ultimatum, threatening to provide
"new incentives" to ensure cooperation, was signed by
the New University Conference (NUC), RL-SDS, and
SACC. However, SACC and the NUC both claimed
that they had been listed without authorization.

[33] *Technology Review,* June 1970.
[34] *Ibid.,* February 1970

On January 15, a guerrilla theater performance portrayed several students "suppressed" in cheese cloth. Then the students marched to the president's office to hold a "people's injunction." About 200 students entered a door that had been smashed open by an iron battering ram, and they remained for a "live-in" lasting thirty-four hours. Johnson responded, "I do not intend to negotiate on the basis of an ultimatum or on the basis of an occupation of an office, and I do not intend to provide room and board indefinitely." The atmosphere inside the office was described as "a brotherly-sisterly mood of optimism." [35] By the next evening, the sixty remaining tenants of the president's office left.

During the "live-in," a thousand students and faculty attended a meeting in Kresge Auditorium, and a straw vote indicated that only about twenty approved of Albert's expulsion. Although many radical students had rejected him during the November action, Albert now attracted wide support. Meanwhile, the Institute obtained a court injunction charging twenty-nine persons with vandalism and trespass. Fifty-six complaints were issued against this group, which included 2 members of the instruction staff, 2 from the research staff, 13 students, 3 former students, and 9 others not connected with M.I.T.

Most were put on probation, but George Katsiaficas was also brought before the Third District Court of Middlesex County for disrupting a class by distributing leaflets. He was sentenced to two months in prison and

[35] *Ibid.*

received his B.S. degree while in jail. An extraordinary episode during the trial suggests the public view of the student activities. When Katsiaficas' mother broke down on hearing the sentence, the judge called her up, castigated her for "not bringing her son up properly," and sentenced her to ten days in jail for disorderly conduct.[36]

Final examinations began soon after the January live-in, and student activism subsided. Interest continued to decline, although the UCS tried to reactivate the issues by calling a second March 4. The day was devoted to speeches by scientists, many of whom were active at the government policy level, and who focused on the implications of past arms control policy. No one attempted to call a research stoppage, and SACC did not participate. Its sponsors described the day as "depressing" and a letdown.

The events from November to January had sapped the vitality of the movement. The satire edition of *The Tech* sarcastically announced that M.I.T. planned to break the MIRV contract "as a move to rob the revolution of one of its most important issues." In its place $130 million per year would be contracted to fund an antisubmarine sonic weapons system designed to match the resonant frequency of Soviet submarine hulls and to "destroy them invisibly."

[36] *The Tech*, May 22, 1970.

VII / The Decision to Divest

Confrontation politics during 1969 forced the administration to move rapidly to a decision despite conflicting objectives and constraining budgetary conditions. In controversial situations that require immediate action, decisions tend to be made by a small group of people at the top level of an organizational hierarchy.[1] As pressure increases, decision makers tend to reduce the number of variables they are willing to incorporate into a decision; yet their commitments are likely to be widely accepted. This was the case at M.I.T., which generally has a reputation of being a centrally run institution. After a year of controversy, reduction of conflict became a part of the decision-making objective, and the process indeed became increasingly exclusive. Implementation of the Pounds Panel recommendations was virtually removed from public view; directorship of the Instrumentation

[1] Gene D. Paige wrote of another crisis: "The more the felt need for immediate action, and . . . the greater the anticipated acceptance of a costly commitment, the smaller the decision unit." In "The Korean Decision," James Rosenau (ed.), *International Politics and Foreign Policy* (New York: Free Press, 1969), p. 468.

Lab changed in January 1970 with little publicity, and the administration began to consider the various pressures bearing on the situation.

The University as an Inertial System

There are many factors that militate against change in an institution such as M.I.T., and prominent among these are economic needs. Research flexibility is a luxury contingent on financial security, and it became painfully evident during the academic year 1969–1970 that the prolonged period of generous federal research support was over. Funding was substantially curtailed during this year and further reductions were anticipated. At best the financial prognosis was uncertain. In hard financial times the risk of accountability to sponsoring agencies is increased, a point that became explicit with the announcement in November 1969 of the Mansfield Amendment to the DOD authorization bill for fiscal year 1970.[2] The amendment precluded DOD sponsorship of any research project unless it had "a direct and apparent relationship to a specific military function." This had critical implications for M.I.T., which received $16.9 million from the DOD in 1969 for on-campus basic research. The intention of the amendment was to force the transfer of all basic research funding to civilian agencies. However, university administrators doubted that these agencies could take over existing projects in a reasonable length of time.

[2] Section 203 of the Military Procurement and Research Authorization Bill, November 1969.

Meanwhile, the pressure on universities to give up classified weapons research was increasing. Lee Du-Bridge, adviser to President Nixon on Science and Technology, had stated, "I agree that it is not appropriate for secret military research to be carried on within university campuses. Not many universities do this now, and I would urge others to phase out any classified weapons research." [3] But while many considered military research inappropriate, costly changes during a period of financial uncertainty were an additional burden.

The volume of research at M.I.T. was reduced during 1969–1970 as follows:

Table 7. Research funding at M.I.T., 1969–1970 (in millions) *

	1968–69	1969–70
Lincoln Lab	66.5	64.1
Draper Lab	54	50.1
On-campus projects	55.8	58.3
Total	176.3	172.5

* The following on-campus projects received significant DOD funding: Francis Bitter, National Magnet Laboratory ($3 million); The Center for Material Science and Engineering ($1.9 million); The Research Laboratory of Electronics (12.3 million); Project MAC–Computer Research ($3 million); Cambridge Project ($1.5 million).

Financial prospects were especially bleak for the Instrumentation Laboratory, which released about 200 employees, or 10 per cent of its staff, in 1970 and anticipated

[3] Lee A. DuBridge, "The Social Control of Science," *Bulletin of the Atomic Scientists*, 25 (May 1969), 35.

further reductions. Several long-term missions were in their final stages: Poseidon contracts were to terminate by 1973, the hardware portion of the Apollo system was in production, and laboratory work on the SABRE guidance system designed for the Air Force was nearly complete.

The possibilities for conversion were not encouraging. Trips to Washington generated only a few small contracts, and there were fears that the uncertain future of the laboratory was affecting the decisions of contracting officers. Each project in the I-Lab had its own contracting officer who was responsible to a higher level supervisor for the success of the project. Because immediate decisions on the acceptance of extensions and renewals of projects were partly contingent on the confidence of these officers, their reaction to the campus turmoil concerned several project leaders in the laboratory. In the spring of 1970, a large Poseidon contract was due for renewal. If the laboratory were not allowed to meet Navy requirements that included the controversial "womb to tomb" involvement, it would lose a major source of funds. Officers at the higher levels of the sponsoring agencies did not pressure the M.I.T. administration or threaten to withhold contracts. They felt that in the short run the turmoil had a positive consolidating influence on laboratory personnel and that work was not affected by the Sheehan Committee investigations. Some, however, were nervous over the uncertain future of the laboratory.[4] Foreseeing a separation

[4] Telephone interviews with Rear Admiral Levering Smith, director of the Navy Polaris project, Robert Frosch, deputy

from M.I.T., they were troubled by the potential loss of formal links with the Institute and the expertise of its faculty and research staff.

Pressured by project leaders, Draper continued to demand freedom of action in the I-Lab. The laboratory, he later contended, had always sought civilian contracts and would continue to do so,[5] but his efforts to get involved in projects such as air traffic control had not been successful. He scoffed at the notion that the laboratory had any "political clout" for obtaining research contracts outside its special field, and he claimed that what had been called his "stubbornness" about conversion was based on a realistic evaluation of the funding situation.

Support for Divestment

Meanwhile, by December, active interest in the entire issue appeared to be declining; only about 500 faculty appeared at a December 10 meeting to discuss the Special Laboratories. During this meeting, laboratory representatives asserted they would not have their affairs determined by student and faculty groups. Then, a motion was made by Ascher Shapiro, professor of mechanical engineering, that both laboratories be severed from M.I.T. The details of his suggestion were significant in

---

director in the Office of the Secretary of Defense, and Robert Seamans, secretary of the air force and former deputy administrator of NASA.

[5] As evidence of his own concern with civilian work, Draper cited the Elmer A. Sperry Award he received in December 1970 honoring distinguished engineering contributions to the art of transportation for the successful application of inertial guidance systems to commercial air navigation.

the light of subsequent events. He argued that the educational spillover of the labs was too small to justify M.I.T.'s managerial responsibility and noted that as a laboratory grows in size, it is inevitably dominated by professionals within the organization. Gradually its interests tend to diverge from those of the university. M.I.T. was thus in the position of managing laboratories for the benefit of national agencies such as DOD and NASA. He also felt that as long at M.I.T. continued to receive massive funding for the laboratories, its image would be that of a wealthy organization, making it more difficult to initiate new projects on campus. He saw divestment as a way to open up new possibilities unhampered by old structures. As for the students' hope of capturing the laboratories and denying their resources to the military, Shapiro argued that "as long as the powers of the Pentagon are unchecked, the military research that the DOD wants to get done will get done. . . . It is both futile and wrong to use M.I.T. as a club with which to beat upon the Pentagon." [6]

Divestment would resolve a number of problems for the administration. First, administrators had been concerned about the Special Laboratories for some time. In 1963, President Julius Stratton had given due praise to the "impressive" productivity of the large laboratories but also had noted how the pattern of federal funding contributed to the "charges of opportunism, to the

[6] Ascher H. Shapiro, "A Position Paper on Retention or Divestiture of the Special Laboratories," February 1970 (mimeograph).

directing of proposals toward popular fields, and to the rise of a new class of 'scientific entrepreneurs.' " [7] Concern focused particularly on the Instrumentation Laboratory, and in 1966 a small group within the administration, uneasy with the autonomy and unaccountability of the laboratory and the difficulties in administering it, had begun to explore ways of severing the relationship. At that time the lab could have been sold for a profit, but the propriety of selling a facility that was formally a part of an academic department was dubious, and relationships with the sponsoring agencies dictated caution. Plans were discussed but never pursued.

By 1969 the pressure from faculty and students served as a catalyst, and the economic and political difficulties suggested a solution. Moreover, an organization model for divestment already existed. In 1958, a major segment of Lincoln Lab that had been working on the SAGE (Semi-Automatic Ground Environment) Air Defense System spun off from M.I.T. because of the feeling that further involvement in integrating SAGE with other defense systems would compromise its role as an educational institution. MITRE was incorporated as a not-for-profit systems engineering company with about 88 per cent of its dollar volume in military work. The core of its staff included 250 engineers and scientists who transferred from Lincoln Laboratory; by 1968 with 901 technical employees and 1,937 total staff, it was larger than its parent organization. Included on its board of

[7] M.I.T., *Report of the President* (Cambridge, 1963), pp. 42–43.

trustees are James Killian, Jack Ruina, and William F. Pounds; thus ties to M.I.T. are formally maintained.

The MITRE experience was available as a promising model. Divestment would allow the laboratory to follow through on its obligations to its sponsors and to maintain the integrity of its research teams. As Shapiro's proposal suggested, it could also be regarded as a way of extending M.I.T.'s capabilities in the direction of social and environmental research areas. In a situation of numerous and fundamental disagreements, divestment now seemed to offer something for almost everyone.

In January 1970, when Miller replaced Draper as director of the Instrumentation Laboratory, he still kept his office at the Urban Systems Lab. According to Draper, at the I-Lab "business has gone on as usual": there was virtually no change at all. The period from January until May, when the decision was made public, allowed the administration time to build up support and to postpone the announcement of a dramatic change in a controversial area until the end of the academic year.

General interest in the issue remained at a low ebb. On February 11, the faculty held a special meeting to discuss the future of the laboratories, but less than one-third of the faculty attended. At the March 11 faculty meeting it was clear that old alignments had not really changed. One group still claimed that the correct interpretation of the Pounds Panel recommendations was that the laboratories be retained; others proposed to speak out publicly against present research on weapons development, and outside the auditorium SACC and a labor union contingent picketed against divestment. But when Shapiro repeated his divestment proposal, it now received considerable attention. With their options limited, laboratory personnel saw divestment as a way of resolving uncertainty; for faculty members it offered a way of preventing further distraction.

A final blow to any remaining hopes for conversion was the decision of the Department of Transportation on March 25, 1970, to centralize its research in the former NASA Electronics Research Center in Cambridge. This decision virtually precluded their funding a conversion program in air traffic control at the I-Lab.

Plus ça Change . . . : The Decision

On May 17, a Boston *Globe* reporter announced that informal sources indicated that M.I.T. would retain the Special Laboratories since the alternative of divestment was too costly.[8] Administrative decision-making was indeed a well protected procedure, for three days later at the final M.I.T. faculty meeting of the year, President Johnson announced the decision, already approved by the Executive Committee (for text, see Appendix III). Lincoln Laboratory would be retained, but the Instrumentation Laboratory would be divested from M.I.T. in two stages. As of June 1, it would be established as a separate and independent division of the Institute with its own board of directors. Johnson estimated that the second stage, that of complete divestment of the I-Lab, would take a year. According to Johnson, his decision

[8] Victor McElheny in Boston *Globe*, May 25, 1970.

was based on five questions: Could the laboratories function under the Executive Committee's directive to limit work on systems intended for operational deployment as weapons? Would money be available to move in new directions that would fully utilize the capabilities of the laboratories; and would the laboratories make that choice if the money were available? Is the Sheehan Committee a workable long-term means of evaluation? Would present and future contractors be able to maintain a reasonable employment level at the laboratories? [9]

Johnson saw but one viable alternative that would preserve both the integrity of M.I.T. and its responsibility to the laboratories and to the national interest. Conversion, he claimed in an interview, was a "misnomer." One cannot decree that people change the direction of their research. "We do not have the right to hurt the capability of the laboratory by continuing to impose a restriction that neither the laboratories nor its contractors are willing to accept." [10] Thus, in May, the relationship between M.I.T. and the laboratory returned to one functionally identical with what it had been prior to the Corporation decision to implement the recommendations of the Pounds Panel. The laboratory could continue to bring in contracts and was no longer subject to review by a university committee.

The divestment plan pertained only to the Instrumen-

[9] Howard W. Johnson, "Statement on the Special Laboratories," M.I.T., *Institute Report*, May 21, 1970. The complete text of this statement is in Appendix III.

[10] Interview reported by Boston *Globe*, May 21, 1970.

tation Laboratory, though the controversy had concerned Lincoln Lab as well. If the two laboratories are
compared, major differences appear that shed some light
on the reasoning behind the decision (see Table 8). Both
the emphasis on scientific publication and the amount of
time spent on research indicate that the orientation of
Lincoln Lab differed considerably from that of the Instrumentation Lab. Lincoln, with stable funding dis-
bursed internally, had considerable flexibility. But the
I-Lab, dominated by large-scale mission-oriented projects, was organized around highly specialized autonomous research teams that work independently of one another. Limited by this structure, the laboratory is unable
to take on small exploratory projects. Karl Deutsch has
observed that "the more rigidly the structures and resources of an organization are committed to any particular set of functions and purposes, the less readily
available are they for recommitment, and the less are the
chances for any rearrangement in the system." [11] The
varying adaptability of the two laboratories was evident
in their different responses to the steps taken by the
M.I.T. administration. The Sheehan Committee reported
that its activities evoked initial uneasiness but no real ob-
jection from Lincoln Laboratory personnel, while those
at the Instrumentation Lab, afraid of jeopardizing their
support, objected strongly to the review. Draper, oriented to large-scale contracts, categorically declared
that funding would not be available for conversion. But,

[11] Karl W. Deutsch, *The Nerves of Government* (New
York: The Free Press, 1966), p. 227.

Table 8. Differences between the Instrumentation Laboratory and Lincoln Laboratory, 1967–1968

	Instrumentation Lab			*Lincoln Lab*		
Average age of professional staff	35.1			38.6		
Median educational level	Bachelors and course work			Masters and course work		
Percent of Ph.D's	5			33		
Number of employees (total) *	1885			1775		
Professional	(800)			(600)		
Supervisory	(160)			(275)		
Clerical	(300)			(300)		
Hourly	(625)			(600)		
Percentage of professional staff publishing various numbers of papers	0 79%	1–5 17%	6–10 3%	0 38%	1–5 31%	6–10 31%
Percentage of professional staff granted various numbers of patents	0 92%	1–5 8%	6–10 0%	0 86%	1–5 12%	6–10 3%
Percentage of staff spending more than 50% of time on research	6%			21%		
Percentage of staff spending more than 50% of time on development	26%			17%		
Character of research	Mission oriented highly specialized, "cradle to grave"			Grants in many different fields		
Administrative relationship to M.I.T.	No steering committee with M.I.T. representatives. Proposals approved by project director, lab director & V.P. for Special Labs.			Proposals approved by Steering Committee, Gov't Advisory Committee (including Air Force & ARPA members), and V.P. for Special Labs.		
M.I.T. Faculty consultants 1968	4			30		
Research assistants 1968	17			22		
Doctoral level theses completed 1968	17			15		
Vulnerability indicators Location	On campus, in M.I.T. or leased property.			17 miles from campus on USAF property		

Table 8. (continued)		
	Instrumentation Lab	Lincoln Lab
Programs	Poseidon singled out for criticism	No special programs singled out for criticism
Sources of support	52% NASA; 48% DOD	100% DOD; a Federal Contract Research Center

Sources: "A Comparative Analysis of the M.I.T. Instrumentation and Lincoln Laboratories," August 8, 1967 (mimeograph), and William H. Matthews, "Some Aspects of Relationships between M.I.T. and the Special Laboratories," May 2, 1969 (memorandum).
* These figures are estimates.

Lincoln Lab director Milton Clauser, thinking in terms of smaller-scale projects, was more optimistic.

The decision was clearly influenced by ambivalent views about Draper himself. Though he was admired for his genius as an engineer and technical manager, his extraordinary independence as an entrepreneur was resented. Referred to by one administrator as the "J. Edgar Hoover of aerospace," Draper was responsible to no one. He refused to be an "organization man."

Finally, an important factor in the divestment decision was the greater vulnerability of the Instrumentation Lab. It was vulnerable for several reasons: its proximity to campus made it accessible to disruptive incidents; its major work, Poseidon, accounting for 20 per cent of I-Lab employment, was the most visible of the controversial projects; and the emphasis on complete systems and operational involvement was considered inappropriate at a university.

Implementation Procedures

Johnson's decision was immediately acted upon by the appointment of a board of directors, which had already accepted membership by the time the decision was announced. This board displaced the Sheehan Committee, which continued to audit only Lincoln Laboratory proposals. The board does not audit or administer proposals for the Instrumentation Lab; nor does it include student members. Headed by M.I.T. Vice President for Research Albert G. Hill, it consists of three M.I.T. faculty who have administrative positions, plus representatives of industrial, banking, and foundation interests.[12] Draper was appointed president pro tempore. When questioned about its representation, the director noted that the task of divesting the Laboratory was a technical one and that there was no reason for representative participation in a "noncontroversial technical matter."

The board meets monthly with the express purpose of devising as rapidly as possible a means of divesting the laboratory that will not involve "major retraction in employment levels at the laboratory [or] a serious loss of capability in what this laboratory has set itself to do and chooses to do in the years ahead." [13]

Essentially, the board was charged with charting a divestment course that would preserve the laboratory relatively intact, but also provide some return to M.I.T. in

[12] See the names and affiliations of board members in Appendix III.

[13] Howard W. Johnson, "Statement," *op. cit.*

order to minimize the financial burden of divestment. The president was asking for a procedure with minimal impact on both the university and the laboratory; the thrust of the board's primary responsibility was to find a mode of existence for the lab that would change its character and its response to its existing missions as little as possible.

The economic problems posed by divestment were overwhelming. M.I.T. fiscal policy was based on an anticipated return from the Special Laboratories at an estimated $7 million annually. The university comptroller estimated that if the revenues from the Instrumentation Lab were lost, on-campus research funds and Lincoln Laboratory would have to absorb $3,800,000 and the teaching and instructional segment of the Institute, costing $1,300,000. Unless there were a dramatic increase in sponsored research funding, unlikely in the context of the budget squeeze, this would involve an increase in indirect cost rates from 51 per cent to 62 per cent for on-campus research, and from 27 per cent to 32 per cent for off-campus research.

According to another estimate, compensation for the loss of the I-Lab would require a 25 per cent increase in tuition receipts or the income from an additional $100,000,000 endowment.[14] With budget deficits of $2

[14] Several faculty from the Sloan School used a statistical procedure to separate attributable costs from total expenditures in multiproduct organizations to calculate the total financial contribution of the Instrumentation Lab to M.I.T. This report concluded that the cash flow from the laboratory to departmental programs was $3,351,000 based on an estimate

million, the university could not contemplate an outright divestment of the lab. Thus, Albert Hill anticipated problems in reaching the second stage of separation within a year. In October 1970, it was announced that divestment was likely to be postponed due to university financial problems; the estimate was extended from one year to about three.[15] The national economic picture also precluded the possibility of raising sufficient capital, estimated at about $25 million, to run the laboratory as a private corporation. An alternative of divesting the lab as a nonprofit corporation and thus qualifying it for capital advances from the government was being considered in early 1971. Whatever the organizational device, the primary requirement was time. Only if the process was to be spread out over five to ten years could the impact on the laboratory and the Institute be minimized.

Response to the divestment announcement varied. An observer at the May faculty meeting noted with surprise the initial lack of reaction from the faculty. People were tired of protest, and the tactic of announcing the decision as a *fait accompli* rather than as a subject for discussion

---

that receipts of the laboratory were $50,247,000 and costs of input were $46,896,000.

[15] In 1970, M.I.T. had an operating deficit of $2 million. President Howard Johnson had committed himself to a three-year projected deficit of $10 million. Divestment was predicted to raise this deficit to nearly $25 million. *The Tech*, October 2, 1970.

was accepted with some relief.[16] The board was established; there was nothing to be done. An ambiguous and disruptive situation was considered closed. According to one journalist, "the most important consequence of the decision was that it removed an enormous distraction . . . [over] an issue which is really less important than how an influential educational institution can restructure its education."[17] And in *Fortune Magazine*, President Johnson was featured in a long supportive article as "the best damned university president in the United States," and Draper as the "inventive genius and master showman." The article referred pejoratively to "the motley crew of student activists" and to Chomsky as the "grand guru of anti-war protest." March 4 was called "purple oratory."[18]

Reaction at the laboratory was ambivalent. Project directors were relieved; their proposals were no longer reviewed and the decision had removed considerable uncertainty about the perpetuation of their research groups. The immediate problem for the project leaders was the survival of these groups, and if this meant sever-

[16] The faculty reaction reflects how a community manages internal conflict. Anthropologists point out that conflict in one set of relationships, if it does not contradict the overriding values of a social system, tends, in fact, to reinforce social cohesion. See Max Gluckman, *Politics, Law and Ritual in Tribal Society* (Chicago: Aldine, 1965).

[17] Boston *Globe*, May 25, 1970.

[18] John Davenport, "Come Squeeze or Bust, in Ho-Jo We Trust," *Fortune Magazine*, May 1970, pp. 176 ff.

ing from M.I.T., so be it. However, the long-range problem of remaining viable was a serious one. Affiliation with M.I.T. provided prestige and encouraged the participation of young scientists attracted by the university. Moreover the nonprofit status as a university laboratory provided a competitive advantage on the contract market. Since many laboratory activities entailed applications of existing technologies which were no longer unique, losing the advantages of affiliation could be disastrous in a competitive situation. It was also feared that divestment would encourage some of the most productive people to leave. While providing short-term relief, the divestment decision created long-term uncertainty.

Some project directors, along with Draper, were bitter, and their resentment was directed specifically at the administration. Though Draper talked of student activists and the UCS with disdain, he emphasized that they were "just a few insecure and irresponsible people" concerned about their own research funding. The administration, on the other hand, should have been more responsible. He claimed that divestment was absurd for a laboratory with no fixed assets but merely expertise. Project directors were annoyed when Philip Bowditch, the education director of the laboratory, talked of strengthening educational ties to the Institute. They felt "kicked out" and were anxious that divestment get under way. If the laboratory could only use the $5 million overhead that went to M.I.T., they argued, it could capitalize itself. And why was Draper the only member of the laboratory on the Institute's board of directors?

SACC's response was curiously similar. The students questioned the motives behind the decision, viewing it as a further example of undemocratic, unrepresentative decision-making procedures. "Why are there no blacks, no women, no labor representatives on the governing board?" They regarded the decision to maintain the functioning of the laboratory as "a cop-out," a politically skillful "Nixon-type operation," which used Draper as a political football in order to let off pressure and put down dissent.[19]

Students expressed their doubts that the laboratory would, in fact, be divested on a time scale "relevant" to their social and political concerns. They viewed the first stage of divestment as a shield, allowing the laboratory, in effect, to resume its former status and to take on new weapons work without even the limitations imposed by the Sheehan Committee. Indeed, in June 1970, soon after the divestment announcement, a proposal for a $3.5 million ULMS missile contract was sent to the Navy. And a year later, in June 1971, two important administrative appointments were announced. Brigadier General Robert A. Duffy was appointed by the board of directors to a newly created position of vice president of the Draper Lab. General Duffy, retiring from the Air Force, was in the Office of the Director of Defense Research and Engineering at the Pentagon from 1963 to 1967, and then with the Space and Missile Systems Organization

[19] *SACC Newsletter,* June 1970.

(SAMSO), first as deputy for reentry systems and then as vice commander. The second appointment was that of John E. Kirk, selected by Draper as his special assistant. Kirk had spent eight years with the Instrumentation Laboratory as a project director for the Titan Guidance System and later as an associate director responsible for the inertial guidance developments required to support the Air Force ballistic missile program. He had worked in the Office of the Deputy Director of Defense Research and Engineering as an assistant director for space technology, and more recently as special assistant for Southeast Asia matters responsible for the analysis of special research and development requirements. In this capacity, he had completed an assignment as science adviser to the Military Assistance Command in Vietnam just prior to his appointment in the Draper Laboratory.

When Johnson claimed that "were we to impose restrictions on the laboratories, we would be wrong," a student replied, "Oh, no you would be right." But fatigue and administrative strategy had successfully dissipated the remaining interest in the case. *The Tech* ran several editorials; some indicated relief, others saw the decision as a failure. The tone was one of a letdown: the assumption that the university was a flexible institution, that it might shift its own priorities in order to play a significant role in challenging national priorities was now realized by activists as extraordinarily naive. On May 27, 1970, the satire edition of *The Tech* sarcastically announced that "due to financial considerations, the best interests of the future of the Institute dictated that an immediate end to undergraduate education is necessary for M.I.T. to successfully continue its appointed tasks in society." [20]

Temporarily at least, the laboratory conducted its work as before, except for the significant fact that a board of directors rather than Draper alone was in charge of the laboratory. The administrative decision, intended to accommodate as many interests as possible, pleased few. A major distraction was removed; but the questions raised by the critics were not resolved.

[20] *The Tech*, May 27, 1970.

VIII / Universities and the Ethic of Responsibility

Paul Goodman saw the events of March 4 as the beginning of a kind of "religious transformation" which called into question the entire relationship of science, technology, and social needs. "For an attack on the American scientific establishment is an attack on the world-wide system of belief." He described March 4 as a "surge of localism, populism, and community action" in the face of big science and an interlocking of technologies and institutions. "A mighty empire is stood off by a band of peasants and neither can win." [1] It is perhaps no accident that "conversion" became the key word for those seeking change at M.I.T., and that SACC defined conversion as "not so much a change from one function to another, as from one framework of total experience (lifestyle, life purpose) to another." [2]

The M.I.T. activists directed their political agitation toward pressuring the administration to take decisive

---

[1] Paul Goodman, *New Reformation: Notes of a Neolithic Conservative* (New York: Random House, 1970), pp. 3, 23.

[2] *SACC Newsletter*, December 3, 1969.

action that would alter the research orientation of the Institute. They based their demands on the principle that scientists and engineers must make value judgments about the social implications of their work. The burgeoning of new organizations of politically active scientists calling for "social responsibility," "reordering of priorities," "advocacy in the public interest," and "science for the people," all reflect the acceptance of this principle by increasing numbers of scientists. Activists at M.I.T. hoped to force the institution to assume a moral position.

But the issues raised by activist demands at M.I.T. were not easily resolved. While individuals may engage in moral politics, institutions have particular constraints. Moral criteria, as highly generalized prescriptions of the way behavior *ought* to be shaped, permit diverse interpretations: [3] institutional decisions tend rather to be influenced by concrete objectives, specific interests, and material needs. And these too may be interpreted in moral terms: indeed M.I.T.'s decisions were justified in terms of *obligations* to employees, *commitments* to contractors, and the *right* of an institution to hurt the capability of a laboratory.

What happens when scientists and science students try to translate their concerns about the use of science into political action directed to changing national priorities? What channels are available for influencing political decisions? And what are the obstacles to the success of such activity? To consider these questions, let us analyze the

[3] Werner Levi, "The Relative Irrelevance of Moral Norms in International Politics," *Social Forces,* 44 (1965), 226–233.

political assumptions and tactics of participants in the M.I.T. events, and the institutional constraints that ultimately determined the decision to divest the Instrumentation Laboratory.

Political Expression at M.I.T.

Ironically, universities create their own difficulties by training students to view their environment critically. As a part of the students' environment, the university inevitably becomes a vulnerable target. Indeed, the issues raised by March 4 had fundamental implications for the Institute and, more generally, for the changing role of scientists with respect to the government and society.

During periods of uncertain transition, both those groups seeking change and those supporting an existing situation need to state their positions and justify their actions. In fact, one of the most striking aspects of the events at M.I.T. was the incredible proliferation of paper. The quantity of print produced by students, faculty, administration, and interested persons outside the university was overwhelming. At first the administration encouraged the widest possible expression of opinion, which resulted in the 26 volumes of Pounds Panel hearings, 247 position papers, and the "Agenda Days." This input was intended to provide a rational basis for decision. Activists, on the other hand, saw no possibility that rational dialogue would lead to the decision they felt to be appropriate, for they viewed the question of research priorities at M.I.T. in a political perspective in which rational debate is of limited relevance.

Seeing no alternative to overt political action, they engaged in confrontation politics that brought into play a totally different use of dialogue and debate.

Confrontation, a tactic borrowed from the civil rights movement, defies the symbols and expectations of an existing relationship; both the research stoppage, with its implications of trade-union-type pressure and, later, the threat of violence during the November Action, violated the expectations of the academic community. While the administration operated in terms of hearings and panels, committees and commissions, discussions and dialogues emphasizing the "community of M.I.T." which "belongs to each of us and to history," SACC and SDS bargained and demanded as interest groups "confronting" the administration.

Confrontation tactics, intended to draw attention to a dissident viewpoint, rely heavily on language, both for shock value and to counter established assumptions implicit in the language of those they challenge. Draper's speeches referred to victory and defeat. He talked of "respected traditions among nations," "progress in military technology," "rationality," "peaceable resolutions," "freedom," and "tranquillity" (see Appendix I). For the activists, these phrases contradicted reality; maintaining peace through developing the "potential for destruction" was as ironical as a "clean bomb" or the infamous statement concerning the annihilation of Bien Tre: "It became necessary to destroy the city in order to save it." Equating peace with military power was viewed in Marcusian terms: "The organs of the established order admit and advertise that peace is really the brink of war, that the ultimate weapons carry their profitable price tags. . . . In exhibiting its contradiction as the token of its truth, this universe of discourse closes itself against any other discourse which is not on its own terms." [4] Manipulative use of language, referred to by one literary critic as "totalitarian rhetoric," [5] is a verbal device that juxtaposes words with opposing emotive connotations. If peace is identified with military power, this precludes further discussion.

The students at M.I.T. rejected the entire set of established assumptions implicit in the language of weapons development; they redefined the "rules of the game" for their own purposes. When asked about his own use of language, Michael Albert described the way people in power define and use words by quoting Herbert Marcuse: "Obscenity is not a picture of a woman who exposes her pubic hairs, but that of a fully clothed general who exposes his medals in a war of aggression. Obscenity is not the ritual of the hippies, but the declaration of the high dignitaries of the church that war is peace." [6]

Students spoke in terms of demands and ultimatums, emphasizing the theme of "science for the people" and, significantly, insisting on a distinction between the "people" and the "government." One of many posters,

[4] Herbert Marcuse, *One Dimensional Man* (London: Sphere Books, 1968), pp. 78–81.

[5] Frank D. McConnell, "Vietnam and 'Vietnam': A Note on the Pathology of Language," *Soundings*, 51 (1968), 195–207.

[6] Michael Albert, quoting Herbert Marcuse, *The Tech*, April 16, 1969.

placed on the Instrumentation Lab, read: "Building con-
demned under Article 2, people's code. All properties
used for oppression are to be confiscated and returned to
their rightful owners, the people." [7]

By talking in terms of ultimatums rather than rational
discussion and using a language of nonnegotiation, dissenters provoked a response. That their rhetoric initially
served to stimulate a wider dialogue suggests that under-
neath their verbiage, the students had raised an appropriate issue.

According to one observer of student movements,
Theodore Lowi, the analysis by radical students of the
character of university activities is "astonishingly appropriate."

The students were first to . . . articulate the fact . . .
[that] services in the contemporary university are essentially policies, that policies involve collective choices, that
collective choices involve advantages and disadvantages in
the struggle for rewards that society has to offer, and that
such struggles involve power, which is the very opposite
of the ideal of education. . . . In their own innocent way,
students have actually been trying to hold the university
to its own pretensions.[8]

Indeed, the main thrust of the activist movement was
based on values very similar to those often expressed by
the M.I.T. administration, that science and technology

[7] Slogans on walls, on posters, and on leaflets were important both for radicals and for their critics; one slogan appeared as follows: A $\int$ SDS equals ½ ASS.

[8] Theodore J. Lowi, *The Politics of Disorder* (New York:
Basic Books, 1971), p. 125.

should respond with greater commitment to "problems of human significance." But despite this agreement on a general level, the issues could not be resolved. Student demands conflicted with interests and expectations long established at M.I.T. on the basis of existing research priorities.

Institutional Constraints

"The evolution of the laboratories over many years has yielded a spectrum of expectations and obligations which involve individuals and organizations both inside and outside the M.I.T. community," noted the Pounds Panel.[9] The administration was responsible for balancing these interests and for maintaining internal order and financial solvency. Despite philosophical agreement with many of the principles expressed by activists, it was unable to respond to their substantive demands: administrative options were limited by institutional imperatives.

First of all, conversion from military to civilian technology in some cases would mean a shift from research at the leading edge of advanced technology to work that involved the application of existing knowledge; from a situation of virtually unlimited resources to one of uncertain and limited support; and from an area in which M.I.T. has a major influence in defining national policy to one involving numerous political and social obstacles.[10]

[9] M.I.T., Review Panel on the Special Laboratories, "Final Report," October 1969, p. 7.

[10] For a comprehensive analysis of the problems and implications of conversion see Seymour Melman, *The Defense Economy* (New York: Praeger, 1970); Marvin Berkowitz, *The*

Second, the administration was forced to deal with strains within the Institute that were aggravated by activist tactics. An academic community sustains a delicate tension among many groups. Strains exist between faculty and nonfaculty; between "insiders" who have contacts with Washington and "outsiders"; between those with grants and those with needs. Draper and other I-Lab personnel saw faculty members of the UCS as a group of jealous professors concerned with their own funding difficulties. Working on practical problems with relatively stable funding, they looked down on the nonprofessional and inefficient aspects of campus research often diverted by educational goals. On the other hand, remarks from faculty denigrating the scientific sophistication of laboratory engineers were abundant.

Part of this tension, revealed during the crisis, is rooted in the history of M.I.T. Its rapid evolution from a technical school to a diverse, science-based university left a degree of internal resentment. Engineers are labeled by some scientists as conservative, and they, in turn, resent the increasing dominance of the discipline-oriented scientist, a point that was clearly evident in Draper's sensitivity to the "disrespect for endeavors directed toward real world results as compared to basic science" (see Appendix I). In the context of these strains, the ad-

Conversion of Military-Oriented Research and Development to Civilian Uses (New York: Praeger, 1970); and Ellis R. Mottur, _Conversion of Scientific and Technical Resources: Economic Challenge—Social Opportunity_ (George Washington University, Monograph 8, March 1971).

ministration felt it important to define what constituted appropriate university activity by distinguishing between "exploratory work on new systems concepts," on the one hand, and "developing operational weapons systems based on these concepts," on the other.[11] But in the most controversial area of advanced systems technology of concern to the military, this distinction can be a delicate one and, in any case, it ignores the question of intended technological application.

A further problem in responding to demands for change is that many commitments in a university are made by individuals or by departments. Scrutiny by an administration is viewed as interference, as a threat to academic freedom. Johnson himself defined a university as a refuge "where any individual can pursue truth as he sees it without interference by any man or group." [12] Outside direction by the administration, as well as by students, is accepted only with reluctance. The faculty at M.I.T. has often tended to be more conservative than its administration, a fact which has tended to increase the reluctance to accept administrative interference.[13]

Finally, the challenge to the university to take a corporate position on political matters posed a dilemma that was illuminated in a brief exchange between two faculty members. Attempting to prevent a vote on the faculty

[11] President Howard W. Johnson, Statement on the Special Laboratories, October 22, 1969 (see Appendix II).

[12] *Technology Review*, October 1969.

[13] During the sanctuary dispute, for example, several administrators sided with the AWOL soldier, while that same year 80 per cent of the faculty endorsed ROTC.

position on MIRV, a physicist said, "It ill behooves a university faculty . . . to vote on matters outside of its area of competence." But a member of UCS replied, "If not us, who?" [14] It was difficult for the faculty to respond to this challenge, even in the face of widespread disillusionment with the military use of technology, for even the UCS, as a group, was ambivalent when it came to turning its own academic institution into a battleground over government policy.[15] Clearly, the university is not a community with one representative voice, and therefore finds it difficult to respond as a corporate entity to major institutional challenges.

M.I.T., more than many other universities, lives with the recognition of its relationship to the "real world"; indeed, it was the scope of its involvement outside the university that led activists to argue that the claim of political neutrality was a myth; that even the acceptance of given research priorities is an act in support of a particular political system. The administration's decision to divest the Instrumentation Lab and its subsequent dif-

[14] This exchange was between Professors Jerry Zacharius and Philip Morrison.

[15] SESPA representatives appeared at M.I.T. in January 1971 and asked M.I.T. faculty to sign a pledge not to participate in war research, and to counsel students and colleagues to do the same. The UCS members who were present refused, noting the difficulties of taking an absolute position in the light of the complexity of the defense problem. They objected to SESPA tactics: "Signing such a pledge is a matter for personal conscience, not collective intimidation," See *Science*, January 15, 1971, and the letter from Lee Grodzins in *Science*, April 15, 1971, in response.

ficulties in implementing that decision illustrate how organizations, such as the laboratory, based on a given set
of research priorities carry their own impetus as interests
develop that depend on their perpetuation. Abstract concepts of "social responsibility" tend to be outweighed by
these specific interests. But conflict concerning the direction of technological research is inevitable once a university assumes a public service role in which its output is directed explicitly to the needs of society. For
societal needs are themselves in conflict, and with no
accepted system of social ideals that would define an appropriate use of technology, universities are necessarily
exposed to the politics of competing interests and dis-
cordant demands.

Appendix I / Contrasting Assumptions of C. S. Draper and the Activists

The views of Charles Stark Draper, embodied in the policies of the Instrumentation Laboratory, contrast sharply with the perspectives of M.I.T. activists. These differences are indicated in the following excerpts from speeches and articles.

On the Use of Science and Technology

Charles Stark Draper

Bound by the diverse problems of modern society, the only possible long-term hope for mankind is to use the capabilities of systems engineering for providing technological means to control the overall circumstances of the human environment.[1]

Technology is not either good or evil, beneficial or destructive; it merely gives men capabilities for realizing situations closer to their own desires through modification in existing states of nature.[2]

Technology is not an enemy of Social Evolution, rather it provides tools of great power that should be used—not destroyed—by Sociologists and Humanitarians. If humanity is to survive and advance it must be served by wise agencies that enjoy substantial confidence from concerned and dedicated people who hope to improve living conditions for everyone on earth.[3]

[1] Charles Stark Draper, "Systems Engineering and Modern Technology," *Engineering Education*, 60 (April 1970), 810.

[2] Charles Stark Draper, "Military Technology and the Future of Mankind", M.I.T., September 1970, p. 41 (mimeograph).

[3] *Ibid.*, p. 6.

The Activists

Science and technology have a powerful impact on society and on history. Those who develop science and technology have in their hands a powerful weapon of destruction and a major instrument for overcoming the problems of contemporary society.[4]—Noam Chomsky.

It is increasingly less possible to believe that scientific advance is defacto social progress—e.g. that producing an ABM is defending the free world, stopping communism, or helping people to a better life.—SACC.[5]

The extent to which "technology is value free is hardly very important given the clear commitments of those who apply it. The problems with which research are concerned are those posed by the Pentagon or the great corporations, not, say, by the revolutionaries of Northeast Brazil, or by SNCC. An activity that produces on demand the techniques of exploitation is not neutral in application. Science cannot be separated from the will that controls it. You don't retreat to the laboratory and produce pure science in today's America. You do the research for which you can get funds.—SACC.[6]

[4] Letter from Noam Chomsky to Dean William Pounds, May 10, 1969.
[5] *SACC Newsletter*, September 17, 1969.
[6] *Ibid.*

On Technological Decisions

Charles Stark Draper

Decisions to develop certain areas of technology or to employ available technology, are, in general, made by people and agencies different from those directly concerned with advancing technology itself. . . . Pioneering projects and production activities selected for technology to carry out are determined by conclusions of the Decision Makers. . . . Once tasks have been established and provided with adequate support, scientists, administrators, engineers . . . all cooperate toward the objective. . . . Sociological, political and moral forces must be evaluated and taken into account by the Decision Makers, but considerations of this kind should not be allowed to effect activities at working levels. Chaos tends to appear under an environment in which each worker develops his own opinions as to the morality of his particular task and unilaterally refuses to continue his efforts if his personal reactions are negative.[7]

Certainly, the highest forms of rationality are required. . . . Unfortunately such rationality is not a natural capability of many individuals. Rather it must be developed by years of experience and careful education in science and engineering. Placing responsibility on individuals qualified through such preparation insures that plans and actions will be determined by knowledge and reason rather than emotional reactions.[8]

[7] Draper, "Military Technology and the Future of Mankind," *op. cit.*, p. 16.

[8] Charles Stark Draper, "Technology, Creativity, and the Changing Social Environment" (Kettering Award: Washington, D.C.), October 29, 1970 (mimeograph).

The Activists

Through its actions in Vietnam, our government has shaken our confidence in its ability to make wise and humane decisions. . . . The response of the scientific community to these developments has been hopelessly fragmented. There is a small group that helps to conceive these policies, and a handful of eminent men who have tried but largely failed to stem the tide from within the government. The concerned majority have been on the sidelines and ineffective. We feel that it is no longer possible to remain uninvolved.—UCS.[9]

Intellectuals are in a position to expose the lies of government, to analyze actions according to their causes and motives and often hidden intentions. . . . It is the responsibility of intellectuals to speak the truth and to expose lies. . . . Should decisions be left to "experts" with Washington contacts—even if we assume that they command the necessary knowledge and principles to make the "best" decision, will they invariably do so? And a logical prior question, is "expertise" applicable, that is, is there a body of theory, and of relevant information, not in the public domain, that can be applied to the analysis of foreign policy?—Noam Chomsky.[10]

We must emphasize that political and historical judgments are critical even in what appear to be technical matters, that there are no experts qualified to deal with these general issues, and that public policy is a reflection, to a very significant extent, of economic power that is entirely removed from the democratic process.—Noam Chomsky.[11]

[9] Union of Concerned Scientists, "Petition," *Bulletin of the Atomic Scientists,* 25 (March 1969), 8.

[10] Noam Chomsky, "The Responsibility of Intellectuals," *New York Review of Books,* February 23, 1967.

[11] Noam Chomsky, "Personal Addendum," in M.I.T., Review Panel on Special Laboratories, "Final Report," May 31, 1969.

On M.I.T. and the Role of Universities

Charles Stark Draper

The Institute as one of the organizations that enjoys the benefits provided by the United States must contribute its fair share in areas of its particular capabilities to the survival and progress of our nation. A basic part of this contribution is that of furthering the . . . respect among nations of the earth at a level high enough to insure international tranquility. . . . If science, technology and other regions of activity are controlled by political decisions rather than the traditional customs of academic freedom, the Institute runs a great risk of descending into a state of mediocrity.[12]

Educational institutions have not generally responded in any systematic way to the overall need for a broad and sound coverage of science, applied science, humanities and engineering coupled with a simultaneous fostering of the positive and constructive mental attitude that is of fundamental importance for the successfully overall practice of technology. . . .

Teachers, themselves neither engineers or technologists, tend to build up disrespect for endeavors directed toward real-world results as compared to basic science, where any concern for applications of knowledge to the achievement of specific results is specifically disclaimed.[13]

[12] Charles Stark Draper, "A Position Paper on the Special Laboratories," M.I.T., February 20, 1970, p. 5 (mimeograph).

[13] Charles Stark Draper, "Technology, Engineering, Science and Modern Education," *Leonardo,* 2 (1969), 151.

The Activists

M.I.T. is concerned with doing what the "proper authorities" want done, not with deciding what should be done. Once that decision has been made (and who decides which authority is "proper"?) M.I.T. provides the technical and managerial skills to do it. . . . M.I.T. cannot be understood in isolation from the scientific community or from U.S. society as a whole; . . . it reflects the values, practices and problems of capitalist America. The character of the channeling process at M.I.T. is such that one is put on a conveyor belt into the military industrial complex.—SACC.[14]

The major contribution that a university can make to a free society is by preserving its independence as an institution committed to the free exchange of ideas, to critical analysis to experiment, to exploration of a wide range of ideas and values, to the study of the consequences of social action or scientific progress. . . . The university betrays its public trust . . . if it merely adopts and limits itself to policy determined elsewhere.—Noam Chomsky.[15]

The things M.I.T. is doing are direct dangers to peace, to justice for oppressed peoples, and to the survival of humanity. The immense resources of the Institute must be turned from death and destruction to work for the benefit of man. —SACC.[16]

[14] *SACC Newsletter,* September 17, 1969, p. 1.
[15] Noam Chomsky, "Personal Addendum," *op. cit.,* p. 34.
[16] *SACC Special Newsletter,* May 26, 1969, p. 7.

On Military Technology

Charles Stark Draper

Significant differences of technology used by rival sides have been the factors that, during the course of history, have determined the victors in many conflicts. . . . Progress in military technology has become so great that any country failing to keep its developments and equipment in step with new capabilities can no longer expect to maintain a respected position among the nations of the earth. . . .

Because it is impossible to set down in advance the exact requirements for success in any endeavor of warfare, while failure may be attended by disaster, projects in military technology are selected with care and systematically carried through with highly concentrated efforts to provide considerable margins of performance based on the best available judgments of the agencies responsible for favorable results in possible confrontations.[17]

[17] Charles Stark Draper, "Military Technology and the Future of Mankind," *op. cit.,* p. 11.

The Activists

Increasingly the need for new military technological advances has been exaggerated, resulting in the development of unnecessary weapons systems. . . . Too often has the concept of national security served as a carte blanche for bankrupt and sometimes tragic policies. . . . We urge you to promote scientific endeavor not for its military potential, but for its potential to alleviate human suffering; not "from the point of view of international prestige," but from the point of view of science as a cultural achievement.—SACC.[18]

[18] Letter from SACC to Lee DuBridge, January 14, 1968.

On World Peace and the Future of Mankind

Charles Stark Draper

Peaceable resolutions of international disputes must finally come from discussions of fundamental issues by groups of well educated, able individuals . . . entrusted with real responsibilities in forming decisions for the governments they represent. To receive genuine consideration . . . these governments must be generally respected because of their existing capabilities. . . . The capabilities involved are of two kinds: those of the mind . . . and those of existing and advancing technology. . . . Paradoxically, the only practical means for preventing technological destruction or technological conquest of the earth is the continuation of pioneering developments in the technologies of major competitors to maintain a mutually recognized balance of respect high enough to restrain the eruption of major violence, . . . in which the potential for destruction is so overwhelming that the other side must concede defeat rather than to try conclusions in a hopeless conflict. . . . This pattern based on progressive technology surely represents the only way that is now apparent to determine the future of mankind.[19]

Technological developments leading to capabilities that increase respect for any nation actually favor stability. . . . There is no chance of controlling the course of events by . . . forbidding progress from further research and development.[20]

[19] Draper, "Military Technology and the Future of Mankind," *op. cit.*, p. 32.
[20] Draper, "A Position Paper on the Special Laboratories," *op. cit.*, p. 4.

The Activists

Any vestige of security which the present situation affords would be destroyed by the U.S. deployment of MIRV . . . the possession by the U.S., of a first-strike capability would be disastrous. . . . We are now at a time when arms limitations are possible. The Russians clearly seem to want to proceed with limitations agreements and have realized certain of their conditions regarding inspections. . . . Indeed the deployment of both offensive and defensive missiles can largely be monitored by satellite. But the MIRV changes this, since one cannot be sure how many warheads an enemy rocket might contain. . . . This constitutes a major escalation of the Arms Race. It threatens the possibility of arms limitation. . . . We believe that these weapons deeply undermine the best interests of society. Deployment of MIRV may very likely destabilize the strategic arms race and thus imperil the future of civilization itself. . . . We oppose the genocide that the U.S. is perpetrating in Vietnam and which these weapons help to make more efficient. —SACC.[21]

[21] SACC, *Special Newsletter*, May 1969, p. 19.

Appendix II/ *Statement by President Howard W. Johnson on the Special Laboratories, October 22, 1969*[1]

Members of the Faculty:

I believe in the accountability of the President of an educational institution to his several constituencies, and I also believe in the necessity of mutual understanding and expression of support by a faculty if its President seeks with your help to formulate and carry out policy.

I come to you to seek your views and support for today and the days that follow, on a vital question—one affecting our policy on the two special laboratories in the months ahead. That support is a necessary condition for what we hope to accomplish.

I regard the issue of the two laboratories as critical to the future of the Institute, and this meeting may be the

[1] M.I.T., *Institute Report*, October 24, 1969.

most important we'll attend for years to come. We face conditions where it is vital that there be close rapport and confidence between administration and faculty with full awareness of the complexities of agreement in such a large and diverse institution.

Let there be no mistake about it: we are at a point of policy change in our direction of the laboratories.

What we do should reflect M.I.T.'s interests as *we* best understand them. In that way and no other, will we make the greatest contribution to education, to the wise advance of technology development, and to the basic strength of this country.

I am well aware of the government's interests, the interests of the sponsors, and those interests are important. I believe that what I propose takes their interests into account. But they may not see it this way, and they may want to do something differently. Since the agencies of the government, by their ownership of equipment and the sponsorship of contracts, initiate, in vital ways, the work of the laboratories, they have that right. The support of the sponsors is a necessary but not sufficient condition for what I now propose.

I am especially aware, too, of the interests of the laboratory personnel, that distinguished team of engineers and scientists, and I am aware of the changing views of the members of the laboratory. Their right to take individual action in terms of their perception of the situation is also clear to me. Their integrity must be protected and while what I propose today I believe to be in their interests, they may conclude differently. The support of the laboratories is a necessary but not sufficient condition for the approach I now propose.

These are rights that the sponsors and members of the laboratories have. I recognize and respect them.

But I do know that I have the responsibility for speaking for M.I.T.'s general interests in these matters, and we would not permit our policy to be set by outside agencies or even by special interests groups within the Institute. And obviously the much less qualified views of outsiders—the voices of the far left or the far right—will not determine our policy.

We have before us now some considered views on what we should do as policy for the labs. We now have the final report of the Review Panel, available to me last weekend, and now printed and available to you at department headquarters offices, and at the Institute Information Center (7-111). The majority report of the Review Panel is essentially the same as the report issued by the whole Panel last spring. Its conclusions are essentially the same four recommendations of the first report:

1. To continue defense related research, but to shift substantially the balance of the work of the laboratories in the direction of domestic and social problems.

2. To seek to declassify a substantial portion of the work of the laboratories recognizing the classified defense research will continue.

3. To develop more effective ties between faculty and students and the laboratories.

4. To set up a Standing Committee "as a means of providing the President with the considered advice of students, faculty, and laboratory staff" relating to the work of the laboratories. "At the same time, this Standing Committee could provide a useful means for informing and involving the community in laboratories' programs. . . .

A second function of the Standing Committee—that of reviewing existing programs—has [been] performed in part by this Panel." [2]

Additionally the Panel recommended that the Poseidon-Polaris project was inappropriate for the laboratories and that while present commitments were to be honored, we should examine that program. For the sake of clarity, let me tell you here of the status of those programs.

We have three principal contracts with the Navy on Poseidon and Polaris. So no one can make a greater mystery of it, essentially there are three contracts, two of which conclude in September of next year, one which continues until December of 1973.

A fifth recommendation was added in the final report—that the entire matter of the relationship between the Institute and its two special laboratories be reviewed on a regular basis.

The force of the deliberations of the Panel last spring was that all 22 members signed the report, some obviously reluctantly. Now four members have disassociated themselves from the conclusions. Two additionally concur, but say as they did last spring, that divestment of the labs may eventually be necessary. But 18 members of the Panel support its final recommendations—a strong base for consideration by all of us.

Last month an important recommendation was made by the Executive Committee of the Corporation. The Committee accepted the recommendations of the Panel and endorsed an interim program of implementation. The statement of the Executive Committee is as follows:

[2] Quotations from pp. 19, 20 of the "Final Report" of the Review Panel.

"The Executive Committee and Corporation have accepted the preliminary Pounds Panel recommendations and endorse an intensive program of implementation, recognizing that M.I.T. has existing obligations and responsibilities and recognizing full well that available funds for new programs and new directions take time to generate.

"The Executive Committee of the Corporation believes that it would be inappropriate for the Institute to incur new obligations in the design and development of systems that are intended for operational deployment as military weapons. This is not to mean that with its unique qualities the Institute should not continue to be involved in advancing the state of technology in areas which have defense applications.

"The Executive Committee of the Corporation feels that the matters involved in the preliminary Pounds Panel recommendations should have the President's high priority and should have a major claim on his time in the next few months."

As I mentioned at our September Faculty Meeting, Professor John Sheehan has accepted the chairmanship of the Standing Committee, and the following members have agreed to serve: Professor Peter Elias, Professor Robert Halfman, Mr. David Hoag, Professor Edward Merrill, Mr. Walter Morrow, Professor Carl Overhage, Professor Hans-Lukas Teuber, and Mr. Michael Marcus, graduate student.[3]

I would like to see the fundamental recommendations of the Review Panel achieved: first, I want very much to see our work applying high technology to domestic and social

[3] On October 23, Andrew Gilchrist was nominated by the Undergraduate Assembly and appointed to the committee.

problems expanded in the labs just as it has on the campus, and the directors of the laboratories feel the same way. To this end I have pressed hard and continuously for a major foundation grant; I have approached the Executive branch of the government, and have had discussions with many members of the Congress, government agencies, potential sponsors of various kinds. And so I would like to see that fundamental recommendation achieved.

Second, I would like very much to see our work in basic technology related to defense continue—and I believe it is important to the future of this country that such work continue. I intend to ask the Department of Defense for a substantial fund for the support of basic technology related to defense. Let me describe what I believe the new policy means regarding operational weapons systems and it will be further detailed as we deal with cases in the future.

The Special Laboratories will continue to do fundamental research and to develop new technology in the fields of communications optics, guidance and control, radar systems, geophysical systems, and computer design and applications. The laboratories will continue to do exploratory work on new system concepts including those with important defense applications. However, the laboratories will not assume responsibility for developing operational weapon systems based on these concepts, nor will either laboratory assume responsibility for the field testing or production of specific weapon systems.

This policy does not preclude the assumption of total system engineering responsibilities in defense systems other than weapons and in other fields such as space, medicine, transportation, education or urban systems if it should appear to be desirable to do so.

To make the matter completely clear I would like to examine some examples of past activities of the Laboratories.

The Instrumentation Laboratory has excelled in the development of precision electromechanical instruments for navigation and position measurement purposes, among them gyroscopes, accelerometers and navigation computers. The Laboratory also pioneered in the integration of these components into highly accurate systems. This work, including the building and testing of experimental systems, would be continued in the future; however, the development and production engineering of a guidance and control system to be part of a military weapons system, such as the Poseidon or Polaris missile, is regarded as inappropriate for the future.

The assumption of total responsibility for the guidance and control systems—such systems as Apollo and the Deep Submergence Rescue Vehicle—is not precluded and will be decided on the basis of the merits of a specific project.

The Lincoln Laboratory developmental activities have been concentrated in the fields of communications, radar development and apparatus for data acquisition and processing. The program of the Laboratory also includes a broad mixture of fundamental and non-directed research, advanced component and development and analytical work in systems development. The Laboratory has done pioneering work on many systems including the SAGE Air Defense System, the BMES's Ballistic Missile Early Warning Radar, scatter and satellite communication systems and a large seismic nuclear test monitoring system. It has not, since its early days, accepted responsibility for production engineering or production supervision of such systems.

Experimental systems work of the type previously carried out at the Lincoln Laboratory remains appropriate for the future.

I would hope that in the laboratories, with this framework, every man who has been working on basic technology related to defense and domestic problems would have the opportunity to do so.

I say I would like to see these fundamentals of the Review Panel's recommendations achieved. But it must be said that we are pursuing the most difficult of courses in which there can be no instant success. The feasibility of these two interlocking goals—basic technology related to defense and domestic technology—will take some time to test. We must find out if the money is available or likely to be in the budget for 1970–71. We must find out if the ideas for large-scale technical involvement in domestic problems can be expanded in this country.

In the meantime, I must tell you there are other complications. At the very time that we seek to expand into domestic area, it is already clear that quite apart from our own wishes in the modification of the work in the laboratories, we fully expect that there will be cuts in federal defense research expenditures now affecting Lincoln Laboratory and the Instrumentation Laboratory.

In summary, I ask for your support at this critical juncture to pursue a test of the Review Panel recommendations. I know many of you have problems with those recommendations. They are either too soft or too hard. Many of you doubt they can be financed. I think we have to test out these propositions.

I and my associates need to explore fully the implementation problems of the Panel's recommendation: the basis on which we continue our efforts related to defense technology, the basis on which we can expand our domestic commitment in the laboratories, and their relationship to the campus. It would be unfair to the labs to presume we can do these things without testing whether the money is in fact in sight to support the new balance of activities.

My judgment is that it will take the rest of this academic year to be able to appraise the prospects for large funding for non-defense funding prospects of the labs in these areas. And, also, the continued availability of funding for defense technology that we are willing to accept. It is only in the light of our full understanding that I will be prepared to propose the course recommended by the Review Panel to the faculty and to the Corporation. I will ask the laboratory heads and their associates for their support for this year on this basis.

In closing, I say again that it would be a defeating proposition and a serious mistake to allow the labs to hurt their overall effectiveness without making sure we can make the principles behind the Panel's recommendations work. It would be better to separate the labs completely sometime in the period ahead than to reduce their effectiveness in every way by presuming the plan would work, only to find later that it cannot, either by lack of your support or that of the labs or the funding availability beyond our control. We cannot exclude that possibility of separation.

It must be said, too, that hasty and inadequately considered action would have serious and negative effects on the financing of every research project on the campus.

And so on this basis, I ask for your support now on a course of action which I propose to enter over the remainder of this year—to test the feasibility of the Panel recommendations and the Executive Committee's recommendation. I am not asking for you to approve the Panel recommendations. We have to discuss that in the months ahead. Maybe it will be the will of the faculty that the Panel recommendations should be moved one way or the other but we ought to test out their feasibility. And this is what I am asking you to do in approving a program of a test of the Panel's recommendations and the feasibility of their application to the labs. That, it seems to me, is only fair to the labs and to M.I.T. During this period there would be full opportunity for the faculty to enter into discussions which we must have on this vital issue. In May I would plan to account to you, to report fully my recommendations for further faculty discussion.

I seek now your expression of support, essentially your confidence in the wisdom of this course. There are, of course, detailed issues that must be worked through, but I seek your support by a vote at this time for the course of action I have outlined.

Appendix III / Statement by President Howard W. Johnson on the Special Laboratories, May 20, 1970[1]

Members of the Faculty:

I want to report to you today on the decision that I have had to reach in connection with our two laboratories. In October, and again in March, I reported on the framework within which I felt I had a responsibility to decide the direction of our policy and action in relationship to the two large laboratories. This faculty and the laboratories have given me support for this course, for which I am grateful. In the seven months that have passed since October, I have tried hard to listen to every voice and read every word relating to your views, I participated in discussions with faculty, students, and members of the Special Laboratories staff. I have considered every plan. I have done so conscious

[1] M.I.T., *Institute Report*, May 21, 1970.

of the grave responsibility surrounding M.I.T.'s actions—
a unique responsibility for education in the advance of
technology. I have tried, as I have said before, to reflect
M.I.T.'s interests. In that way and in no other will we
make the greatest contribution to education, to the wise
advance of technology development, and to the basic
strength of this country.

Today I report my action. There are those who would
wish we could delay forever this difficult decision point.
No one is more conscious than I of the difficulty, the complexity, and the sadness surrounding this point. But delay
and indecision will serve no one. I have made the decision,
and I report it to you now. I have acted, and you have the
responsibility to hold me accountable.

I thought there would be several alternatives as I considered this intensely complicated subject with all of our
responsibilities to so many people, to the complicated inter-
relationships of our faculty, students, staff, and the broader
world of technology, and our responsibility to the country.

I now think that there is only one viable alternative. I
think there is one way that preserves the Institute's integrity and preserves our responsibility to our laboratory
associates. I have based this decision on several tests:

A. Could the laboratories function under the Corporation
   Executive Committee's directive which barred new
   work related to systems intended for operational deployment as military weapons and the Standing Committee's review as set by the Review Panel's Report
   of last spring.

B. Would the money be available to move in new directions that would utilize and match the capability of
   the laboratories to their fullest extent.

C. Would the laboratories make that choice, were it available.

D. Is the Standing Committee of the Laboratories a workable idea in the long run in terms of the capability of the laboratories.

And, finally,

E. Would present and future contractors of the laboratories be able to work with us to maintain a reasonable employment level, a major responsibility for us in those two laboratories.

I conclude that M.I.T. can continue to manage Lincoln Laboratory in essentially the same frame as we have in the past into the foreseeable future. I conclude that we cannot over the period of the next months and years continue to manage the Draper Laboratory under the restriction of the Corporation Executive Committee's directive.

Let me repeat, I believe we can continue to manage Lincoln Laboratory applying the framework that I have cited to its activities and relationships including the Standing Committee's advisory function; progress in the declassification of projects; and closer educational ties with the Institute. To the extent that there are inconsistencies and difficulties, I believe they can be resolved in full and equal collaboration, and I believe the educational opportunities represented by the relationship between the campus and Lincoln Laboratory, as well as through related service, continue to be real and genuine.

I conclude that we cannot continue to take that responsibility for the Draper Laboratory under the restriction of the Corporation Executive Committee's directive without major retraction in employment levels at the laboratory and without a serious loss of capability in what this laboratory has set itself to do and chooses to do in the years ahead. I do not believe that we have the right to hurt the capability of the laboratory by continuing to impose a restriction that neither the laboratory nor its contractors are willing to accept. Were we to force that situation, we would be wrong, and it would not work.

As you know, the fundamental emphasis and styles of the two laboratories—the central tendencies of their approach to projects—differ. Further, unlike the Lincoln Laboratory, where a single contract and a longer period of time for adjustment makes the framework of support that we propose possible, Draper Laboratory has neither the funding prospect nor the time frame to work through the necessary three-to-five-year change. The funds and the time are not there. To pretend they are will only do basic harm to the laboratory, its concept of how to apply advanced technology, and it would force an unfair end to an unstable situation.

It would clearly be irresponsible for M.I.T. to allow this to happen. To hurt the Draper Laboratory either by indecision or indirection would hurt the fundamental integrity of the Institute and all of us in it. It would be a disservice to ourselves and to our colleagues in the laboratory and to the country that looks to it as a shield.

Accordingly, I have proposed, as I must legally, to the Executive Committee and to the Corporation, and the Corporation has voted approval for, a divestment—to take place in two steps—but clearly a divestment that protects this national asset, its personnel, and the Institute.

The first step will begin immediately—June 1—and the cost will be high. The first step is to establish the Draper Laboratory under that very name—the Charles Stark Draper

Laboratory—as a wholly separate and independent division of the Institute but with its own Board—a Board to be composed of one member of the Corporation, members of the faculty and of outside persons who have a general public interest and experience. The Board appointed by the Executive Committee for a term of one year would elect its president and chairman. The president, pro tempore, named by the Executive Committee would be C. Stark Draper. I have asked the following to serve this one year term, and they have accepted.

Robert A. Charpie, President, Cabot Corporation; C. Stark Draper, Institute Professor Emeritus and President Pro Tempore, Charles Stark Laboratory, M.I.T.; Albert G. Hill, Vice President for Research, M.I.T.; Carl Kaysen, Director, Institute for Advanced Study, Princeton, New Jersey; James McCormack, Director, Communications Satellite Corporation; Charles L. Miller, Director, Urban Systems Laboratory and Associate Dean of Engineering, M.I.T.; Emanuel R. Piore, Vice President and Chief Scientist, International Business Machines Corporation; David W. Skinner, Vice President and Vice Chairman, Polaroid Corporation; Robert C. Sprague, Chairman and Chief Executive Officer, Sprague Electric Company; Mark C. Wheeler, President, New England Merchants National Bank of Boston.

One additional public member has not yet responded to my invitation.

The responsibilities for the interim support of the laboratory would be in the hands of this Board. Operating independently and without the terms of the Corporation Executive Committee's directive, the Board would have the specific responsibility for the seeking in as rapid and short a time as possible the wise and complete separation of the laboratory. I am not sure how long this period of the first step would take. I think in terms of one year. Others, perhaps more aware of the complications, say it will take months longer, some say shorter. But this first step is a necessary step toward an organization that separates in a way that protects the rights of all the employees in the laboratory, that allows for some resorting of tasks and individuals, that allows for the taking over of administrative functions, that allows for the funding of the necessary working capital of the new organization, and that, most of all, allows for an effective choice of the form of the new independent body.

I must tell you that with the final divestment step will come the full burden of the loss of the financial connection with the Institute. Some financial consequences will begin to be felt immediately, without doubt. The impact on the research programs and on the teaching support programs of the Institute will fall on every aspect of our effort. I don't see any way to escape this hard fact. I think it is out of honesty to the laboratories and to ourselves, however, that we take this step.

I think this decision is a fair one. It will continue the educational relationship among individual professors and students connected with the Draper Laboratory during this first divestment period. We give the students involved that assurance. In the second stage, any such relationships would be those with a completely outside organization.

I have asked the Chairman of the Faculty and the Dean of Engineering to form a faculty body which will deal with the educational continuities and discontinuities of this changing relationship.

Professor Charles L. Miller, who has served as Director of the Draper Laboratory, will continue his duties as Associate Dean of the School of Engineering and Director of the Urban Systems Laboratory. It will be Professor Miller's responsibility to continue to develop the Urban Systems Laboratory as a main focus with which new mission laboratories will evolve which will be concerned with a wide variety of societal problems.

I am interested in emphasizing that final, general point. M.I.T. belongs at the edge of the new and broad opportunities of a developing technology. We have played key roles in the past and will continue to do so in the future. Now new ones are emerging and must add in time to the emphasis that has been given in the past to defense-related efforts. M.I.T. continues to depend on mission-oriented research for education and for the development of science, which is, I remind you, a part of our charter. Our decision today continues our commitment to research related to the security of this nation. But, it is clear to me that, largely, these new emphases in medicine, in environmental quality improvement, in the urban fields, will require wholly new agglomerations of faculty and students and staff in laboratories created by their special interest and talents. The money is not today available, but it will be, I am sure, when we look at a longer time horizon. And in time these new laboratories too may need to be allowed to go their own way.

That summarizes my purpose in this report. I hope you will help me make this difficult task of change possible, mindful, as I believe we have been, of the responsibilities of M.I.T. I welcome your questions. I do not seek your approval of the details. I hope you will give me your support on the basic direction of this decision.

A Note on the Program on
Science, Technology, and Society

The Cornell University Program on Science, Technology, and Society is an interdisciplinary program for teaching, research, and increased public understanding. It evolved from a concern with how scientific discovery and technological innovation are changing economic and political institutions and are altering the values that influence social behavior. The program is funded by the National Science Foundation, the Sloan Foundation, the Henry Luce Foundation, and Cornell University.

This book is the third in a series developed within the program to provide information on scientific and technological advances and on the ways in which important decisions about them are made. Each study deals with a specific case selected to reveal the complexity of situations in which the problems and challenges of technology are an issue, and each study treats in detail the broader implications of the individual case.

A number of common themes will be emphasized throughout the series: the use of science and technology to meet public needs, incentives and constraints on the direction of scientific and technological development, and the control of unintended and undesirable consequences of science and technology. We shall consider, in relation to each of these themes, the social and political behavior of various groups: scientists and technologists in the political-governmental system acting in situations which carry them beyond their technical expertise; legislators and policy makers, forced to make decisions often on the basis of inconclusive evidence; and the public, concerned with the implications of technology, whose interest and activities are likely to bear increasingly on public policy.

FRANKLIN A. LONG, Director
RAYMOND BOWERS, Deputy Director

Abbreviations

AAAS—American Association for the Advancement of Science
ABM—Anti-Ballistic Missile
AEC—Atomic Energy Commission
ARPA—Advanced Research Project Agency
CBW—Chemical and Biological Warfare
DDRE—Office of the Director of Defense for Research and
    Engineering
DOD—Department of Defense
DOT—Department of Transportation
DSRV—Deep Submergence Rescue Vehicle
DSS—Deep Sea Submergence Vehicle
FAS—Federation of American Scientists
FCRC—Federal Contract Research Centers
FFRDC—Federally Funded Research and Development Centers
HEW—Department of Health, Education and Welfare
MIRV—Multiple Independently Targeted Reentry Vehicle
MIT-SDS—M.I.T. branch of Students for a Democratic Society
NAC—November Action Coalition
NASA—National Aeronautics and Space Agency
NIH—National Institutes of Health
NLRB—National Labor Relations Board
NSF—National Science Foundation
NUC—New University Conference
PSAC—President's Scientific Advisory Committee
RL-SDS—Rosa Luxemburg Students for a Democratic Society
SACC—Science Action Coordinating Committee

SAMSO—Space and Missiles Systems Organization
SESPA—Scientists and Engineers for Social and Political Action
SINS—Submarine Inertial Guidance System
SIPI—Scientists' Institute for Public Information
UCS—Union of Concerned Scientists
ULMS—Under-Sea Launching Missile System
USL—Urban Systems Laboratory
VTOL—Vertical Take-Off and Landing Control System
YAF—Young Americans for Freedom

Index

Library of Congress Cataloging in Publication Data
   (For library cataloging purposes only)

Nelkin, Dorothy.
   The university and military research.

   (Science, technology, and society)
   Includes bibliographical references.
       1. Massachusetts Institute of Technology.   2. Military re-
   search—U.S.   3. Education, Higher.
   I. Title.   II. Series.
T171.M49N4 1972   355.07'09744'4   74-38285
ISBN 0-8014-0711-7